Advanced Leadership Insights

How to Lead People and Organizations to Ultimate Success

Advanced Leadership Insights

How to Lead People and Organizations
to Ultimate Success

Edited by

Wolfgang Amann
HEC Paris School of Management

and

Katja Kruckeberg
International Leadership Consultant

Information Age Publishing, Inc.
Charlotte, North Carolina • www.infoagepub.com

Library of Congress Cataloging-in-Publication Data

CIP data for this book can be found on the Library of Congress website:
http://www.loc.gov/index.html

Paperback: 978-1-68123-816-6
Hardcover: 978-1-68123-817-3
E-Book: 978-1-68123-818-0

CONTENTS

FOREWORD AND ACKNOWLEDGMENTS

Wolfgang Amann and Katja Kruckeberg

Both of us as book editors and chapter authors have been actively engaged in leadership development for almost 2 decades. We have seen leadership development change and individual leaders grow, perform, evolve, and at times, fail. What we have noticed over the course of the years is the need for fresh insights on leadership so that individuals and organizations can prepare for current and future challenges. You as the reader will find an integrated collection of emerging thoughts on how individuals can lead themselves to ultimate success, on how to lead others to peak performance and on how to direct entire organizations to a better place.

While we have integrated our own thinking into this book, we compiled this resource on advanced leadership insights with the help of dear and much respected colleagues in order to offer you an even more excellent and varied "buffet of ideas." All of us chapter authors work internationally as we are well aware of the partly culture-bound nature of leadership and management. All of us are more than theorists working in the proverbial ivory tower. All of us have successfully convinced clients of the value of our lessons and insights. With compiled this book the practicing leader in mind. This is mirrored in the writing style of our chapters and the frequently added application exercises. As book editors, we express our gratitude toward our colleagues and fellow chapter authors who have significantly contributed to this volume. We are equally grateful

Advanced Leadership Insights: How to Lead People and Organizations to Ultimate Success
pp. vii–viii
Copyright © 2017 by Information Age Publishing

to our clients, both individuals and organizations of all types and sizes, for their valuable feedback over the years. They helped us identify the needs for further leadership insights as well as what works in specific settings.

Simultaneously, we express a word of caution. While this book is full of insights, success recipes, and fresh patterns, they all need to be adapted to one's personality type, values, skill level, situation, and specific challenge, as well as, aspirations. Also, we noticed that the field of leadership is in flux. We find inspiration from all types of authors and organizations located in different parts of the world. This global competition of ideas might well lead to consequences. First, their shelf life will be limited as new ideas will emerge in the near and midterm future. Second, this will encourage and invite you as the reader to continuously update yourself with regards to latest insights and solutions. Only then can you stay ahead of the game. Not all fashions and trends add value, but the potential must be screened regularly. We, thus, hope to meet in you as the reader a true lifelong learner. We hope you enjoy our collection of advanced leadership insights and wish you success in actively experimenting and applying them.

INTRODUCTION

Wolfgang Amann and Katja Kruckeberg

PURPOSE OF THE BOOK

Alexander the Great was one of the greatest military leaders the world has seen. His tutor in the 4th century BC, Aristotle, shared that an outstanding leader must have three characteristics: ethos, pathos, and logos. Ethos referred to the moral character as a source of ability to persuade and to inspire. Pathos prescribed an ability to touch feelings and therefore move people. Logos required the ability to intellectually convince people—with a compelling reason (Rashid, 1989).

We continue to be firmly convinced of this trio of traits. Yet, in today's world, a fourth attribute seems to become even more pressing—the ability to learn. While ancient Greece and warfare surely had its challenges back then, today's world is by no means less overwhelming.

- Politically, we see the rise of populistic democrats and a precipitating wave of antiglobalization voices in a variety of countries.
- Technologically, we see disruption through digitalization. For example, nontraditional players will occupy 40% of market share in the financial services globally within the next 10 years.
- Artificial intelligence is advancing rapidly, winning the most complex board game, "Go" against world champions, and seeing the first artificial intelligence robot recently passed the entrance exams of a Japanese university.

Advanced Leadership Insights: How to Lead People and Organizations to Ultimate Success
pp. ix–xv
Copyright © 2017 by Information Age Publishing
All rights of reproduction in any form reserved.

- Ethically, we continue to have tremendous challenges in our board-rooms as the recent example of Volkswagen demonstrates. The company illegally installed an engine software manipulation emission tests and reacted with denial when caught.
- Macro-economically, the highest valued financial technology firms are now found in China, not in Silicon Valley or Wall Street. We see that the global economic centers are shifting.
- On the corporate level, most strategies are not implemented as planned. A large part of mergers and acquisitions do not deliver the intended value and most employees around the world are disengaged. According to our research, 90% of staff members do not even know the relevant part of the strategy, nor do they have the energy and focus to effectively implement them.

In such dynamic, interdependent, and ambiguous contexts, leaders must still demonstrate ethos, pathos, and logos. However, learning is the new name of the game. We have therefore compiled this resource of latest insights on advanced leadership. We aspire to support leaders in their quest to rapidly and effectively learn about latest trends in leadership. We have done so by making additional observations on board. We noted that overall levels of busyness among leaders and managers are very high. There is competition for attention. Sources of inspiration, therefore, need to be precise, easy to absorb, and quick to read. This book presents its reader with a series of new insights on advanced leadership that ultimately lead people and organizations to success. Included chapters are short so that the reader can spend sufficient time reflecting on the content. Furthermore, we understand that even leadership experts often only have a few new ideas to represent. Thus, we have teamed up with a group of bona fide experts, all accomplished in their fields, in order to compile this resource. We invite you to read selectively based on your interests and learning needs. All chapters clarify objectives and summarize the highlights in the end. As the English philosopher Herbert Spencer adequately put it, "the great aim of education is not knowledge but action," all chapters in this book encourage immediately exploring how to best use its content. The following section outlines the structure and content of individual sections of the book.

STRUCTURE OF THE BOOK

The "buffet" of ideas we prepared for you has three distinct parts, and we welcome you to self-service the items most interesting to you. The first part of the book deals with leading yourself to ultimate success. The unit of analysis for which we propose fresh insights is thus the individual leader.

Konstantin Korotov is the author of the first chapter, where he provides an overview of essentials regarding a leader's self-development. A thorough leadership development journey has clarity in one's motivation to lead. As this motivation might change over time, Korotov suggests critical reflection in regular intervals. He encourages current and future leaders to better understand why taking on an active leadership role is attractive, and distinguishes several scenarios. There is no right or wrong answer, although more recently concepts of servant leadership have gained popularity. A servant leader is not oriented toward maximizing power, fame, and monetary returns. In contrast, a servant leader gets energized and is motivated by the positive impact of their service to others.

Korotov equally stresses that leaders need to explore and understand the cost of leadership. Beyond decorative titles, higher pay, and influence, there are responsibilities, tradeoffs, and sacrifices. There are many crises to manage over a leader's tenure. If leaders do not understand their own motives, personality, and cost of leadership, dreams and aspirations can turn into nightmares. One of the more dangerous scenarios can entail burnouts, from which only a small percentage would eventually recover. Korotov furthermore reflects on the very beliefs that good leadership stands for. Industry standards may differ from corporate and personal criteria. Not all companies build competencies effectively. Also, the questions can emerge regarding who should take a leader's development further? And who could be held accountable in case things go wrong? Korotov continues by encouraging more leaders to actively request feedback in order to facilitate the learning journey. Significantly aligned with Herbert Spencer's philosophy, that action counts more than knowledge, Korotov encourages experiments to see how feedback lead to improvements.

Katja Kruckeberg's ensuing Chapter 2 investigates the question how leaders can enhance their presence. What are the three key dimensions of presence within one's leadership style? In a comprehensive review, Kruckeberg distinguishes emotional, physical, and mental presence. Her thoughts are initially descriptive, and become prescriptive in the second half of the chapter. Kruckeberg supports her claims and suggestions on how to become a more impactful leader with a series of anecdotes. The book chapter integrates elements from breathing techniques as well as tai chi, neuroscience, and emotional intelligence. Kruckeberg's primary claim is that great leadership leads to more impact and well-being.

Jim Shipley has two contributions in this book. The first one is Chapter 3, where Shipley deepens the insights to be gained from neuroscience in order to enable effective leadership on an individual level. He critically reviews built-in thinking traps and outlines how they can render a leader's life and functioning more difficult. Shipley, thereby, does not view the reality of built-in thinking traps as fatalistic. In his view, the negative impacts of thinking traps can be managed and self-awareness is the key to get started. Shipley outlines the role of humility and active experimentation when trying to improve as a leader.

Shipley adds further thoughts on successful leadership by pointing to mindfulness, a concept that gained substantial popularity around the world. His Chapter 4 builds on the observation and assumption that our brains have a limited capacity to focus our energy and attention. Great leaders are aware of this limitation and they tend to focus. Once again, self-awareness receives center-stage position in Shipley's chapter, and when reviewing a leader's impact, he posits that a stronger focus of energy and attention entails better results. Shipley outlines exercises in order to deal with common distractions for leaders. Leadership can mean different things over time. Leaders motivate, steer a coach to name but a few tasks. Mindfulness can enhance the effectiveness of all of them.

Part II of the book deals with the question of how to lead others to ultimate success. The focus thus moves beyond the individual level. Katja Kruckeberg opens the section by reviewing five success factors of high performance teams. She revisits why teams continue to be crucial and what factors account for a dysfunctional team. Kruckeberg subsequently presents a five-level framework based on her many years in leadership consulting and development. The team efforts will become more impactful as these five levels are mastered and aligned with each other. Kruckeberg includes brief assessments and reflection exercises in the chapter, so that the reader can immediately apply the quantum of the chapter to their setting.

Matthew Mulford authors the next chapter and outlines negotiation skills for leaders. For some, business is nothing but negotiation, and negotiations take place constantly. Suppliers and buyers negotiate. Unions, or individuals, and human resource directors negotiate. Superiors negotiate with their subordinates and vice versa. According to Mulford, excellent leaders need to develop effective negotiation skills. This requires an integration of several skills and topics. The materialistic and financial side must be well understood. Reading people and comprehending the situation is key to effective negotiation. The dynamics of human interactions have to be understood along with the many ways in which to optimize them over time. Leaders in this field, Mulford argues, are not born but made. Negotiation skills can be learned and honed over time. If leaders adopt key concepts and semantics, such as "best alternative to a negotiated agreement" and "zone of possible agreement," they can drastically accelerate the preparation and implementation phases of negotiations.

In the subsequent chapter on reflective leadership by Felix Mueller and Ragna Kirberg, the authors begin by reviewing the world we live in. They also explain why people react with different levels of confidence when confronted with challenges. Indeed, today's complexity can easily overwhelm, and therefore it needs to be understood. Reflective leadership, specifically reflection by thinking and feeling, can help make progress in this regard. The authors offer substantiated advice on how to rapidly acknowledge stress and change one's mental stance toward it. Reflection does not only come in the form of self-reflection. Reflections are also social and joint processes as well, if leaders are ready to open up. Showing vulnerability, ensuring transparency and embracing feedback can bring about solutions which are unreachable for solitary fighters who try to resolve all problems on their own. Authors include a series of reflection and application exercises at the end of the chapter to enable readers with immediate application and experimentation in the presented content.

Wolfgang Amann adds his thoughts on one additional innovation in the field of leadership in the following chapter. Blue ocean strategy has revolutionized the field of strategizing and innovated what is taught in executive education seminars on strategy. Is a similar revolution about to take place in leadership seminars and practice? The chapter outlines what the blue ocean strategy suggests and how it can lead to overcome one of the biggest leadership challenges of today: disengaged staff members. There is indeed more to the concept. It questions the use of psychometric tests, as they are expensive (which often need coaches in addition to faculty members for a thorough debriefing), and the considerable time required in order to lead to change. There may be faster alternatives, although these alternatives can make leaders feel uncomfortable at times.

Part III of the book deals with leading entire organizations to ultimate success. Katja Kruckeberg joins forces with Naysan Firoozmand in order to outline how to navigate complexity on an organizational level. Together, they presented 10 golden principles for chief executive officers assuming leadership roles. The chapter clarifies the role of preparation before starting a new assignment. It sheds light on the first 100 days when a new leader establishes a brand. Kruckeberg and Firoozmand highlight the brevity of the window of opportunity, before staff members assume all would stay the same. The authors emphasize the importance of stakeholder management in order to create value. They clarify the role of trust and credibility when aligning stakeholders. In sync with the overall theme of the book, the authors also illustrate the importance of continuous learning and management of one's energy.

Wolfgang Amann then adds his experience and thoughts on real stake-holder dialog and overall corporate diplomacy. When leaders are confronted with crises, they have to be take a fundamental stance toward being a "nice guy," a "lonely fighter," a "stealth bomber," or a "good citizen." Leaders ought to be prepared for the adversity they will inevitably encounter during their tenure. They need to have proactively honed their diplomacy and stakeholder dialogue skills as the chapter posits.

This book integrates a very contemporary trend as well as challenge. Ruth Ann Lake and Cristina Bombelli investigate women in leadership in the following chapter. The authors review aspirations, obstacles and opportunities. While women have effectively assumed leadership positions in many settings, Brazil, the United Kingdom, Germany, Bangladesh, to name a few examples which are led by women, many organizations as well as corporations still have not dismantled what our colleague Randy White has labeled "glass ceilings" for women. Many male leaders are not yet familiar with methods that integrate women in their leadership teams. Many are still in need to get accustomed to female leadership—in some cultures more than others. This chapter outlines that both men's and women's leadership ambitions are rather similar. The authors point out that skill profiles homogenize, yet the ability to manage diversity needs to be honed.

In the next chapter, Tamara Carleton, William Cockayne, Andreas Larsson, and Berhard Kueppers devote pages to the question why a radical innovation needs visionary leadership. We undoubtedly live in the age of disruption. Each industry sees established players, business models, technologies, and solutions questioned with bold moves by competitors or new players. They might come from inside the existing industry with no boundaries, but increasingly from the outside. Owners and investors play a dominant role as well. The authors review the origin of big ideas as well as their power. As small- and medium-sized enterprises represent the backbone of many economies, the authors clarify how their wisdom and suggestions apply not only to larger companies but also to the smaller counterparts.

Marios and Vicky Katsioloudes continue our learning journey by positing that leaders need to be change masters. This comes back to the well-established differentiation between transactional as well as transformational leaders. If leaders fail to design, lead, and sustainably anchor change, their own survival is at stake and key stakeholders suffer. Leaders ought to be learners and the need to know more about leadership versatility. Leaders must actively close skill gaps when it comes to change management. The authors differentiate between hard and soft skills, outlining that only the combination and balance make all the difference for successful change. Today's companies probably undergo change more frequently than ever before. Change trajectories are becoming ever more complex. Thus, this chapter offers crucial reflection opportunities on how to practically prepare for future change.

The next chapter written by Tobias Mahr and Bertold Stein sheds light on how to succeed in a political organization. Although companies primarily run on an economic motor, leaders have to admit that whether willing or not they have to adopt and sharpen their acumen with regards to politics. The chapter offers interesting reflection opportunities on core questions, such as whether a value driven people stand a chance or not. The authors also outline the role of authenticity in more or less political environments. They revisit the infamous matrix organization, so popular in the 1990s, and how to succeed in one. They clarify how politics complicate decision making and what options exist when dealing with one's superior. Concluding remarks close the book and its collection of insights on advanced leadership.

REFERENCE

Rashid, S. (1989). *Living with leadership*. Jehlum, Pakistan: Book Corner.

PART I

LEADING YOURSELF TO ULTIMATE SUCCESS

CHAPTER 1

A QUICK GUIDE TO YOUR LEADERSHIP SELF-DEVELOPMENT

Konstantin Korotov

OBJECTIVE

At the end of my leadership development courses, I often get questions about sustaining the momentum triggered by participation in a company-supported executive program. Participants inquire about additional learning opportunities, further courses to take, books to read, and activities to explore. Participants sometimes lament that they receive insufficient support in advancing their leadership competencies, wanting more formalized leadership development offerings from their employers. I also often get questions per e-mails or calls from people who may have read my books and articles and who wonder what to do if their organization offers aspiring leaders absolutely no support in the form of executive education, company-sponsored MBA programs, or internal mentoring or coaching schemes.

Concerning complaints about companies doing too little for their executives, who want more in terms of their progress, my response is: Regardless whether or not your employer offers formalized leadership development programs, you need to take responsibility for your advance-

Advanced Leadership Insights: How to Lead People and Organizations to Ultimate Success
pp. 3–9

ment. After all, expecting that someone should turn you into a leader is rather antithetical to leadership. While it may be easier to acquire some competencies and manage leadership transitions when learning resources are available and the company provides you with corresponding support, learning to lead without all the infrastructure may become a powerful resource for your future support of new generations of leaders.

What follows is a quick guide on how you can start, boost, or sustain your leadership development journey.

Explore Your Motivation to Lead

First, explore your motivation to lead. Why is leadership so important to you? Be as open and frank as possible, even though your answers and the power of thinking through them might well frighten you. You need not share these answers with anyone, unless you need to explore the potential of other people's opinions or reactions. In my view, the readiness to explore uneasy questions is a prerequisite for leadership development. Are you ready? Here we go:

- Why is that you believe you can and should take an active leadership role?
- How will this motivation support your organization's progress?
- What will happen if you don't grow into a leader within the boundaries of your current organization? How will this affect your life?
- How hard are you willing to work in order to achieve progress in your leadership role?
- How will your progress as a leader contribute to the wellbeing of the people around you (your superiors, peers, and subordinates, your clients, your family, your community members, and so on)?

If you feel that taking responsibility, mobilizing yourself and others, and helping people to overcome challenges give you a thrill and increase your energy, you will probably be motivated to look for leadership development opportunities beyond what the company can or want to offer you. However, it is important to visualize how your energy and effort can make your organization better. Affective motivation to lead, or the positive feelings associated with taking or anticipating a leadership role, has been shown by research to be correlated with willingness to search for opportunities to test and stretch one's leadership capacity (Chan & Drasgow, 2001).

The purpose of this exercise, which should be repeated regularly, is to ensure that you're clear about what drives your leadership development urge. Leadership involves agency and personal will, so it may be important to ensure that you want to take the effort to developing yourself into a leader, rather than someone else wanting to develop you. Do you begin to see the differences between wanting to develop and wanting to be developed?

Explore and Understand the Costs of Leadership

It is also crucial to not only feel the thrill of increasing your leadership responsibilities, but to be equally aware of the costs and psychological burdens associated with leadership roles. Observe people in your and other organizations whom you consider to be good leaders and think about the potentially downsides of their jobs: delivering negative news, taking difficult decisions, or being held responsible for the organization's performance, even if the latter is beyond their immediate control. Equally, observe people whom you consider to be poor leaders. How do they handle the negative consequences? Put yourself in the shoes of the people you observe; how you would feel under similar circumstances and under watchful eyes of the stakeholders involved?

You may also want to read about current leaders handling a particularly challenging situation and see what reactions they get from the media, social media, other businesspeople, and even your family. It is also always a good idea to have a discussion with your loved ones about the consequences, including the potential costs, of your leadership progression.

Understanding and accepting the costs of leading—assuming, after this exercise, that you still want to lead—may make going through later tough leadership moments easier, since you will have no access to the psychological excuse of not having known or thought about the less pleasant aspects of the leadership role(s). Research suggests that people who were clear about the positive and negative sides of a particular job or role before engaging in it find it easier to cope with such negativity when they face it, compared to those who remained uninformed before they faced tough realities (Phillips, 1998).

Explore Your Beliefs About
What It Takes to be a Good Leader

You need some guidelines concerning what it takes to be a good leader. Start by looking at what your organization thinks about it. Some companies have pretty sophisticated formalized leadership competencies frameworks. Is your company one of them? If yes, it may be wise to look at the framework in use, since it may serve as a foundation for the organization's assessment and selection of future leaders. However, you may not necessary like what you see, since the models often differ substantially from what the company really needs! Some companies may have a general set of expectations of their leaders, while still others may have given it little or no thought. If the latter is the case, you may want to observe what your organization's unwritten principles for assessing, selecting, and/or promoting leaders are.

Now compare the information you have collected with your own sets of beliefs and expectations about leaders and leadership. Through our upbringing and education, we develop a set of ideas or mental pictures of what it means to be a good leader. Sometimes, these expectations are in line with the organization's written or unwritten expectations, and sometimes not. In the case of discordance, ask yourself if the current circumstances require leadership that differs from the ideal you have in your head. You may then want to explore to what extent you are ready to develop yourself into a leader; this may differ from the idealized picture of an ideal leader you have.

Overall, exploring your leadership ideals and comparing yourself to them, as well as to the observed typical leadership behaviors in your organization is an important element in your leadership development. Research suggests that comparisons of this nature are important for our motivation to lead and develop as a leader (Guillen, Mayo, & Korotov, 2015).

Get Feedback

If, after exploring your motivation to lead, the potential costs of leading, and your beliefs of what good leadership is, you still want to continue with your leadership growth and development, go and seek feedback. Invite people to support you through answering the following questions:

- What do people value you for most for in your organization?
- What are the sources of your personal power? What is there associated with your skills, competencies, or relationships that can serve a foundation for expanding your capacity to influence people?
- What do people believe you should be doing differently or you should stop doing?
- What do people think you should start doing?

Gathering feedback is part of the process. You need to work with the data you get and make sense of it. In some cases, you may have to get further feedback, particularly if you hear something surprising. If you hear negative feedback, use this as an opportunity to practice your resilience. Leadership is often costly to the individual exercising it. As a rule, leaders get much more negative feedback than anyone in follower roles. Learning to manage personal reactions to negative feedback is an important leadership development step. On a practical note, make it a practice to respond to negative feedback by asking for additional information and help in understanding what people mean and how you can use this negative feedback productively.

Acting on the feedback is not the only available option: in some cases, you may choose to continue without modifying anything in your specific behavior, as long as you are ready to face the (positive or negative) consequences of making no change in the ways people see you.

Reinforce Feedback With the Wisdom of People in Your Organization or Beyond

You can then reinforce your analysis from the feedback by exploring the experience and wisdom of people in the organization who are in higher-level positions and who can become your informal mentors. On some occasions, you may want to avoid using "mentor," simply seeking opportunities for informal conversations with people whom you believe can be good sources of information and advice.

Even if you do not have access to experienced individuals in higher-level positions in your organization, you would still be better served if, in your leadership development efforts, you can rely on a sparring partner or someone with whom you can bounce back ideas and explore questions of importance to you.

Peer coaching can become a powerful leadership development opportunity, one you can deploy without the involvement of your organization or any budgets (Korotov, 2008, 2013). All you need is a partner who is interested in sharing mutual developmental efforts. It is crucial to base the relationship with your peer coach on principles of reciprocity, trust, and psychological safety. The person with whom you engage in peer coaching should not be your potential career competitor. Often, it is best to have someone outside your unit or even organization, someone with comparable business experience who is interested in developing their leadership skills. With this person, you could explore your leadership philosophy, discuss the feedback you received, plan possible experimental steps, and evaluate their outcomes—all in the safety of a confidential discussion with a trusted partner.

Seek Opportunities to Experiment

Seek opportunities to take charge, help others, and do something new with other individuals. If your current job does not allow you to experiment with leadership behaviors, look for opportunities in temporary projects, cross, functional teams, or volunteer gigs. Sometimes, you can experiment with your leadership outside the organization: Think about professional associations, political parties, or community groups. Let people around you know that you are on a learning journey and that you want to be a good leader. Ask for support, help, advice, and further feedback.

Think about less experienced colleagues in the organization and how you can help them to develop their professional, interpersonal, and conceptual skills. Helping people grow and develop stretches your own skills: influencing, motivating, encouraging, inspiring, correcting, and protecting others are part of a leadership package.

Challenge the Organization

At a certain moment, you may want to challenge your organization regarding its leadership development practices (or any other important aspect of your company's functioning). Take the lead in supporting others in their growth, ask questions, share your thoughts, and make suggestions. If you are unhappy with how the organization works, and if you are passionate about it, choose making improvement happen as your personal leadership task. Be prepared to face disagreements, doubts, concerns, and, sometimes, counteractions. You will probably experience many negative aspects of taking the lead and trying to bring about change. Someone might call the legitimacy of your efforts and actions into question. When this happens, your previous work on your motivation to lead, understanding of the costs of leading, feedback, reinforcement from wise people around you, and your experimental efforts will be put to use in your practical exercise of leadership.

The experience of leading may encourage you to reconsider your previously developed foundations of leading. This may sound daunting, but if your purpose is to develop, you need to be ready to change yourself. If you make such a choice, you are taking responsibility for your leadership development. If others make that choice for you, even if they send you to a leadership program, you may need to question whether you are really being developed as a leader.

REFERENCES

Chan, K. Y., & Drasgow, F. (2001). Toward a theory of individual differences and leadership: understanding the motivation to lead. *Journal of Applied Psychology, 86*(3), 481.

Guillén, L., Mayo, M., & Korotov, K. (2015). Is leadership a part of me? A leader identity approach to understanding the motivation to lead. *The Leadership Quarterly, 26*(5), 802–820.

Korotov, K. (2008). Peer coaching in executive-education programs. *Training & Management Development Methods, 22*(2), 315.

Korotov, K. (2013). *Peer coaching practice for managers: An executive education companion.* CreateSpace.

Phillips, J. M. (1998). Effects of realistic job previews on multiple organizational outcomes: A meta-analysis. *Academy of Management Journal, 41*(6), 673–690.

CHAPTER 2

LEADERSHIP PRESENCE

The Three Dimensions
of a Sought-After Leadership Quality

Katja Kruckeberg

OBJECTIVES

In this chapter, I explore the three dimensions of leadership presence—emotional, physical, and mental presence—and show how a leader can develop this capacity by providing insights into concepts, practical examples, and easy activities.

MARILYN MONROE, NEW YORK, 1955

When Olivia Fox Cabane, an international keynote speaker and a lecturer at Stanford University, speaks about leadership charisma, she often refers to an incident that occurred in New York during the spring of 1955. The 29-year-old Marilyn Monroe, who had just landed a cover shoot in the then famous *Redbook Magazine*, is at the center of this story. Marilyn hoped that this shoot would help her establish herself as a serious actress.

Advanced Leadership Insights: How to Lead People and Organizations to Ultimate Success
pp. 11–21
Copyright © 2017 by Information Age Publishing
11

On the day, Marilyn sought to prove that she could decide what people saw in her: Norma Jeane, the girl next door, or Marilyn Monroe, the movie star. She claimed she could effortlessly switch between these roles. Switch on: Marilyn Monroe, world-famous superstar in the spotlight; switch off: Norma Jeane Baker, the lovable, but somehow less imposing woman, appears.

And this is exactly what happened: No one noticed her when she walked to Grand Central Station, where part of the shoot took place. She walked through the station, but the commuters seemed not to care. On the train, nobody looked at her. Once back on the street, she turned around and asked the now famous question, "*Now* do you want to see her?" Within a split second, she had transformed into the radiant, recognizable star. Her facial expression changed, her eyes shone more brightly, her body adopted a new posture, and she had the magnetizing presence for which she became famous. A large group of people gathered around her immediately and cheered loudly.

FINDING THE LIGHT SWITCH

This story very impressively shows that we can change the intensity of our presence within seconds and whenever we want to. Other people will then take notice of us, even if our light might not shine quite as brightly as Marilyn Monroe's. However, most leaders I have worked with are surprised at the degree to which they can intensify their presence. If taught how to do this, they can do so with very little effort. In fact, unconsciously we do this quite often: Imagine sitting on your couch at home after a not very good day. You are feeling suboptimal, not completely satisfied with yourself and the world. Your partner is also late for dinner. The phone rings. You rise from the sofa somewhat reluctantly, wondering whether your partner is calling to say that he or she will be even later. You pick up the handset without looking at the display. It is not your partner, but your best friend from school, whom you haven't spoken to for years. Within a split second everything about your appearance changes. You greet your friend energetically. You add, "I'm well. Couldn't be better!" and also feel this. You radiate presence and energy, just like Marilyn Monroe did that day at Grand Central Station. This is one form of presence.

LEADERSHIP PRESENCE

True leaders are present. After more than a decade of working with top executives, I am convinced that developing leadership presence is about the ability to pay undivided attention to the situation in which people find themselves. It is not so much a human trait as a skill that leaders can acquire. Leaders who are not distracted and give us their full attention are perceived as being present. Unfocused leaders might have the formal power, but you may not recognize them as leaders.

THE THREE DIMENSIONS OF LEADERSHIP PRESENCE

Leaders who are present exude calm and authority. This makes others want to follow them.

Thus, being truly present is a basic requirement in order to successfully lead oneself, one's team, and the organization. The key to greater presence is attention—to oneself and to others. Ideally, presence means that leaders are in the here and now with their heart (empathy), mind (interest), and body (energy). Here, I distinguish between emotional, physical, and mental presence. When these three attention types are present, a leader will feel highly active and will act charismatically.

To describe these facets of presence, meet Jason Smith, MD of a business unit of a multinational electronics company. Jason, who had entered

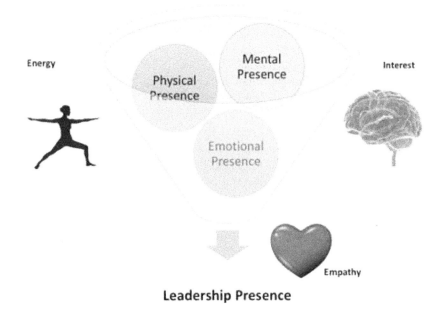

Figure 2.1.

the company as an IT specialist, was appointed MD due to his outstanding cognitive abilities. When I met Jason at a leadership workshop in Paris, we agreed that I would work with him and his team as an executive coach, consultant, and facilitator. Jason's initial goal was for us to work on his effectiveness as a top manager. He believed that when he participated in worldwide upper management meetings some of his less experienced colleagues were listened to more than he was. In addition, aspects of his leadership were criticized in his 360-degree feedback. His team members asked him to take more interest and to be more involved in their work. Jason was very surprised by this feedback. If anything, he was overcommitted to his work. Why did his staff not realize how important his work was to him? During the coaching sessions and the off-site meetings, I noticed that Jason lacked presence on all three of the above mentioned levels.

MENTAL PRESENCE

"One of the reasons why we so rarely find sensible and competent partners in a conversation is that there is hardly anyone who does not prefer to think about what he wants to say next, then to respond exactly to what has been said to him."

—Francois de la Rochefoucauld

When I first read this quote, I felt I had been caught out. As leaders, we are sometimes trapped in our reflections, instead of listening to others. In conversations with Jason, I quickly realized that his mental presence worked as "digitally" as the computer systems that he had learned to control so skillfully. When he expressed his—very elaborate—thoughts, he came across as very present and alive. However, when he was not "on stage," that is, not speaking, his facial expression changed. He seemed absent and slightly negative, which was also why I was initially surprised that he wanted to work with a business coach. He had given no indication that he was interested in the services I provide.

This was also the problem Jason had with others, including his team, the top executive he was struggling with, and the other stakeholders he was dealing with. It was not that he was not interested in what others had to say. The rapidity at which his brain operates simply did not allow him to be in the here and now. Once he had picked up new information, he would immediately process it and would seek to incorporate it into his way of thinking, which prevented him from truly listening.

However, this is a killer for developing and radiating leadership presence. Having presence is not mainly about being interesting oneself, which many leaders mistakenly believe, but about being interested in others. Those who are always "on stage," entertaining others, may initially come across as present. But this kind of presence is short-lived. People do not want to merely be an audience. They want to actively participate and to be regarded as important. If you want to lead others, you need to convince them that you do take them into consideration. Why should educated and experienced people want to listen to and follow a leader who is not interested in what they have to say?

Let us turn our attention to Bill Clinton, who is known to have an exceptional charismatic presence. Experts agree that one of his strengths is to make others feel really listened to regardless of their social status. I once had the pleasure of hearing Mr. Clinton speak at a conference in Geneva. Whatever one may think of him as a person or a politician, he is a fascinating and charismatic speaker. During the speech, I was convinced he had several times addressed me personally. Afterwards, when talking to other people, I realized that many of them thought the same, which amused us. Olivia Fox Cabane (2012) once related what a Republican congressman had said about Mr. Clinton: "I hated him before I met him—I hated him after I met him—but while I met him, MAN, I LOVED THE MAN." He too was captured by this leadership presence.

But let us return to Jason, who struggled with the concept of leadership presence. Jason was not an egocentric, uninterested leader. All his life, he had been accustomed to convincing others with his logical and astute arguments. His analytical intelligence had allowed him to progress. Were he not an exceptionally talented and strategic expert, his one-sided leadership behavior would have affected his career much earlier. A board member, who had long supported him, said that Jason had a reputation as a smartass; a brilliant one, but a smartass nonetheless. According to this board member, this was why the top managers from diverse cultural backgrounds with whom Jason was dealing, found it hard to connect with him. Full presence, and its absence, can be read across cultures; this does not require cross-cultural training.

THE ENEMIES OF MENTAL PRESENCE

Being present is becoming increasingly difficult. The emergence of new, always-on technologies makes us hope that we can become more efficient. Instead, we are becoming increasingly absent. Ironically, our quest for efficiency ultimately undermines our capacity to be fully involved in what we do. Even as we work harder and improve our performance, we are undermining our capacity to create the trust and confidence required for sustainable success (Helgesen, 2016).

THREE STEPS TO CREATE MENTAL PRESENCE

1. We need to be intentional about how we use our time and attention. By respecting boundaries regarding *how* and *when* we respond, we diminish stress, improve our capacity to be thoughtful, and create the conditions needed to manifest an engaged presence. This is not easy, and might require leading upward. Regaining control of *how* and *when* we communicate *with whom* is an essential first step.
2. To avoid mistakes, we need to avoid habitual multitasking. While it's probably impossible to avoid multitasking altogether, it often becomes compulsive, even addictive.
3. We need to recognize that presence requires a purposeful decision and practice (Helgesen, 2016).

MENTAL PRESENCE IN A HIGH PERFORMING TEAM

I work with top management teams from different industries and cultural backgrounds.

During their off-site meetings, which I help facilitate, the top executive leading the team is often the most focused person in the room. However, if you want to turn your management team into a high-performing one (see Chapter 6), the team members' lack of focus is unacceptable. In a high-performing team there are only leaders—everyone should be equally present and focused, not just the person at the top.

PHYSICAL PRESENCE

If circumstances permit, I try to integrate tai chi lessons into my leadership workshops. While not everyone loves tai chi, it is a proven method to hone one's physical presence. During a tai chi session, I instinctively knew how Jason, whose physical presence was very low, would come across. One moment was especially memorable. The tai chi teacher urged us to adopt the warrior pose. This requires you to direct your attention to the middle of your body and to place your feet wide apart, thus stabilizing your body. Your back and head are upright and your arms are stretched out to the sides.

Figure 2.2.   Warrior pose.

I could not believe my eyes: For a moment, I saw Jason's alter ego shining through. His outer appearance changed completely. He looked present rather than distracted, and came across as confident and relaxed rather than overly serious and lost in thought. His facial expression was positive rather than skeptical. He exuded both calm and confidence, a winning combination for a leader. It was as if he had briefly flicked the switch, just as Marilyn had done. Switch on: Jason's leadership presence is visible; switch off: Jason's usual serious and skeptical self emerges. Later, Jason, like many of the executives I work with, made it a personal development goal to integrate similar moments of presence into his business life.

THE THREE ANCHORS EXERCISE FOR GREATER PHYSICAL PRESENCE

A very effective way to change your physical presence is to direct your attention, via the three anchors exercise, to your body several times a day. This is simple to do and can be done wherever you are. Sit or stand upright. An upright posture is a first step toward greater physical presence.

The three anchors exercise consists of three steps:

1. **Grounding:** Ensure you stand on both feet and feel gravity working on your body. If you are seated, feel your bottom touching the chair and your feet resting on the ground. Briefly concentrate on these contact points.
2. **Breathing:** Now concentrate on breathing in and out naturally. Can you relax and breathe in and out with ease? This step is more effective if you combine it with part one of the activity. When exhaling, feel gravity working on your body.
3. **Centering:** Concentrate on the center of your body. Try to breathe from there—just below your belly button.

People will unconsciously notice if you inhabit your body, if you are physically present, or if you just consider your body a vehicle to transport your brain from one meeting to the next. If you experience the inner states of presence, you will also experience a new form of inner balance and wellbeing. Presence is sustainable energy for well-being, since is known to be a regenerative state. Presence increases your leadership charisma, and has overall relaxing effects that are unlike a state of high concentration or focus. Presence is created in the mind, body, and heart. The more you are in the here and now on all three of these levels, the more leadership presence you exude. It also leads to better decision making and better leadership.

EMOTIONAL PRESENCE

Do you remember August 31, 1997? Many people do, perhaps especially women. I too remember what I did that day. I was in Conil, a small Andalusian town on Spain's south coast. When I went to buy a bocadillo (snack) at a kiosk that morning, I was told that Lady Diana Spencer had died the previous night in an accident. This news touched me, as it did millions of people around the world.

Diana's death received the kind of attention that only exceptional people who have done extraordinary things would have received. Like Nelson Mandela, whose political commitment changed the world's political landscape and whose courage touched people.

But what did Diana do that transformed her, the world's most photographed woman, into the queen of hearts after her death? Her charity commitments alone were not the reason for this gigantic wave of sympathy. As laudable as her commitments were, other prominent people have made similar efforts, leading to far less public affection and interest.

In Diana's case, the reason for this adulation was of a different nature: She had a personal appeal that very few people possess to the extent that she did. This appeal is closely linked to leadership presence. What fascinated people so much about Lady Diana was her extraordinarily warm aura, which was evident in her radiant, sympathetic gaze. Her son William seems to have inherited this talent from his mother. They both have an exceptional emotional presence.

INSIGHTS FROM NEUROSCIENCE

Let us explore the concept of emotional presence from a scientific point of view. Research shows that emotional presence is based on a mixture of empathy and sincere compassion, two interlinked concepts. Matthias Bolz of the Max Planck Institute for Human Cognitive and Brain Sciences notes that empathy—the ability to perceive emotions in others and to reflect on them—is the prerequisite for any kind of compassion. In this context, he distinguishes between cognitive and emotional empathy. Prof. Tanja Singer, another expert on empathy at the Max Planck Institute, mentions cognitive empathy, which is when one knows that another person suffers, regards this suffering as bad on an abstract level, but does not empathize emotionally. Emotional empathy refers to the emotional resonance when those neural networks on which the other person's feelings are based, are also activated. This is true compassion, which leads to an associated physical response (Singer & Bolz, 2013).

What happens in the brain during this process was almost accidentally discovered during an experiment with a macaque. Since this experiment, we have known that our empathy and our compassion depend on the number and the functioning of our brain's mirror neurons. Mirror neurons are those that trigger similar feelings in us as the feelings we believe we see in the persons we interact with. This empathy and compassion are present on our face, body language, and voice. In combination with personal confidence, strength, and power—the second behavioral quality of charisma—this leads to a powerful charismatic appearance.

However, compassion can also be faked. Prof. Singer describes an extreme case and refers to a specific type of psychopath—one with a capacity for cognitive empathy, but without the corresponding emotional empathy. These people are sometimes very good at understanding what others need and want. Armed with this presence, they can manipulate others extremely well. These people do not empathize with others and can therefore cause others pain and suffering. Interestingly, these two types of empathy also differ visibly on brain scans. Emotional empathy only arises if one really sympathizes, because it simultaneously creates the motivation to help others and not hurt them (Singer & Bolz, 2013).

The capacity for empathy is genetically determined. However, like other leadership skills, leaders can nourish and develop their ability to empathize. Although this ability may vary, we can expand the capacity to feel empathy during our life. I recommend the book *Cooperation. How Empathy Makes Children Strong* by the bestselling author Peter Høeg. He discusses how we can foster empathy in our children, but the book is just as helpful regarding how to foster empathy between educated and experienced adults.

LEADING WITH EMPATHY

Empathy is critical to leadership development. It is a tool that can lead to hard and measurable results. Daniel Goleman (2004), the author of several best-selling books on emotional intelligence and leadership, identifies three reasons why empathy currently matters for leaders:

1. the rapid pace of globalization (which leads to cross-cultural challenges in the workplace)
2. the abundant deployment of teams (see Chapter 6)
3. the increasing drive to retain talent.

Goleman (2004) points out that leaders with empathy "do more than sympathize with people around them: they use their knowledge to improve their companies in subtle, but important ways." Bruna Martinuzzi (2009), an expert on leading with empathy, shares practical ways in which leaders can nourish their ability to empathize and increase their emotional presence when communicating with their stakeholders:

SIX RECOMMENDATIONS HOW TO INCREASE YOUR EMOTIONAL PRESENCE

1. Truly listen to people. Listen with your ears, eyes, and heart. Pay attention to others' body language, tone of voice, the hidden emotions behind what they say, and to the context.
2. Do not interrupt. Do not dismiss their concerns out of hand. Do not rush to give advice. Do not change the subject. Allow people their moment.

3. Be fully present when you are with people. Do not check your email, look at your watch, or take calls when someone talks to you about their report.
4. Encourage people, particularly quieter people, when they speak up in meetings. A smile can also boost someone's confidence.
5. Give genuine recognition and praise.
6. Take a personal interest. Show people that you care and are interested in their life (Martinuzzi, 2009).

SUMMARY

Being present is the basic requirement for successful leadership. If managers know how to increase their leadership presence, others will be more inclined to follow them. Leadership presence is initiated within a person and can manifest itself at different levels. Ideally, a leader should be present with his mind (interest), his body (energy) and his heart (empathy). Being mentally present is not mainly about being interesting oneself, which many leaders mistakenly believe, but about being interested in others. Emotional Presence refers to a leader's ability to show empathy and sincere compassion. We differentiate between cognitive and emotional empathy. Physical presence requires a leader to inhabit his body. Presence is sustainable energy for a leader's wellbeing.

REFERENCES

Fox Cabane, O. (2012) Speech. [Video file]. Retrieved from https://www.youtube.com/watch?v=LMu_md_5PQ4
Goleman, D. (2004, January). What makes a leader? *Harvard Business Review,*
Helgesen, S. (2016). *What's the secret to leadership presence?* Retrieved from http://www.strategy-business.com/blog/Whats-the-Secret-to-Leadership-Presence?gko=36a1a
Martinuzzi, B. (2009). *The leader as a mensch: Become the kind of person others want to follow.* Six Seconds.
Singer, T., & Bolz, M. (2013). Mitgefühl in Alltag und Forschung. Retrieved from http://www.compassion-training.org

CHAPTER 3

LEADERSHIP AND NEUROSCIENCE

An Inconvenient Truth

Jim Shipley

"Reality is a story the mind tells itself –
An artificial structure conjured into Being
by the calcium exchange of a billion synaptic endings.
A truth so strange it can only be lied into existence.
And our minds can lie. Never doubt that."

—From the computer game *Portal*

OBJECTIVE

In this chapter leaders learn about built-in thinking traps that function to maintain an inflated and arrogant self-image. Neuroscience research suggests these thinking traps are centered in our left-brain. The good news is the negative impacts of our thinking traps can be managed through self-awareness. Humility is the mindset and leadership practice that operationalizes our newfound awareness.

Advanced Leadership Insights: How to Lead People and Organizations to Ultimate Success
pp. 23–36
Copyright © 2017 by Information Age Publishing
23

"COGITO, ERGO SUM"

Human beings possess the greatest intellectual capacity of any known life form. We are able to think, reason, perform root cause analysis, draw logical conclusions, and design elegant theoretical constructs. Many consider our intellectual brilliance the pinnacle of our species: "Cogito, ergo sum" —I think, therefore I am. We pride ourselves—even arrogantly so—in being more intelligent than any other living creature. There is no question that we have a phenomenal ability to think really well!

But we also have a phenomenal need to be *right*! We have a built-in self-grandiosity and driving need to maintain an image of intelligence and competence. The social pressure to be right and accurate—starting in our educational systems and continuing through our corporate business lives—makes it even that more difficult to admit it when our thinking is wrong or inaccurate. We always seem to have a story that conveniently rationalizes our errors to ourselves and to others. This intellectual arrogance is one of the insidious thinking traps that operates in our brain right alongside our intellectual brilliance, especially when things are not going the way we believe they should! This is an inconvenient truth about our minds that we do not like to admit. Our intelligence and competence are not as perfect as we would like to believe.

In some of my leadership development programs I use a classic psychology exercise to offer business leaders a direct experience of how their thinking traps show up. They are invited to test their ability to solve anagrams by rearranging a group of letters to create a common English word. Ten anagrams are presented for 12 seconds each. With this added time pressure, there is a palpable sense of excitement in the air; and everyone wants perform well in front of their colleagues. After asking if there are any questions, the game begins. What they do not know is that only 3 of the 10 anagrams can actually form English words. Thus a perfect score in the game is three, not 10! To add to the confusion and frustration, all three successful anagrams are placed toward the end of the game sequence.

In the debrief that follows, everyone reports that they were positive and focused at the start. But after "failing" to solve the first few anagrams, their attention quickly moved away from the task to how badly they were performing, how quickly they were losing self-confidence, and how fearful they were of being embarrassed. But when questioned further about what else was occurring in their minds, they recognized that they had almost immediately started telling themselves a story to rationalize why they were not doing as well as they thought they should: "I've never played this game before!" "English is not my native language!" "There wasn't enough time!" "You were trying to trick me!" And so on.

These statements may all be true, but they cover up a more important truth: *when people are confronted with circumstances that cause unpredictable results in performance—especially their own!—their thinking can trap them in ways that limit their ability to perform at their best*. The anagram participants thought they were doing badly when in fact most of them were performing optimally. Their *interpretation* of what was happening caused them to lose their confidence, their focus of attention, and to feel bad about themselves. They then fixated on an explanation that allowed them to preserve a positive self-image! Does this sound vaguely familiar to any business scenarios you have been part of?

These "hiccups" in our thinking that are simply a defense for our self-image can wreak havoc in our business decision-making, planning, execution, and interpersonal relationships. How these misjudgments show up in our decision-making have been brilliantly illuminated by Daniel Kahneman in *Thinking, Fast and Slow* (2013) and by Nassim Taleb (2005, 2010) in *Fooled by Randomness* and *The Black Swan*. Kahneman says this puzzling limitation is about

> excessive confidence in what we believe we know, and our apparent inability to acknowledge the full extent of our ignorance and the uncertainty of the world we live in. We are prone to overestimate how much we understand about the world and to underestimate the role of chance in events. (Kahneman, 2013, pp. 13–14)

This chapter is based on the premise that although we cannot eliminate them entirely, we *can* consciously manage our thinking traps by first being aware of how they are wired in our brain and then being more mindful of our thinking process, to minimize the damage these hiccups can wreak in our roles as a business leaders.

TWO BRAINS, TWO WORLDS

To understand how these thinking traps are wired in our brains, we must look at how the two halves of our brain operate and how they relate to the world (see Figure 3.1). Even though they appear to be mirror images of each other connected by a bridge of neurons called the corpus callosum, our left-brain and right-brain process information *radically* differently. We could even say they view reality in completely different ways!

The mystery of why our brain is divided into two distinct halves has long haunted neuroscientists. Recently, however, Iain McGilchrist, in his groundbreaking book *The Master and His Emissary*, offers a compelling hypothesis (McGilchrist, 2012).

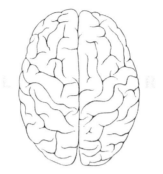

Figure 3.1.   Two hemispheres of the human brain.

He suggests the two halves evolved over millions of years to help manage one of the most challenging and vulnerable moments in any animal's
life—when it is seeking out and eating food. This action requires laser-
focused attention on the potential food source, whether it is a seed on the
ground or another animal to be killed. An animal must then carefully
coordinate all its muscles to physically make the approach, kill—if necessary—and then eat the food. At the same time, it must also be vigilant to
any of *its* predators waiting to do exactly the same to it!

The chances of survival would increase dramatically if there were two
dedicated parts of the brain working in parallel—one focusing entirely on
eating, and the other on avoiding *being eaten*. According to McGilchrist,
this is precisely what our two brains were designed to do.

Thus, the left-brain is focused on seeking, killing, and eating by specializing in:

- laser-focused, goal-driven attention;
- methodical repetition of tried-and-true patterns;
- aggressive, dominating, and tenacious behavior; and
- a confident, positive, unambiguous attitude.

In turn, the right-brain specializes in not being eaten by specializing in:

- broad-focused attention, taking in the big picture, the *gestalt*;
- distractions and the unexpected;
- ambiguity, uncertainty, and complexity; and
- a cautious and defensive attitude.

The two brain hemispheres have evolved with entirely different purposes and operational rules. And as human beings came onto the evolutionary scene, our two brains specialized further.

The right-brain is masterful at social relationship skills, empathy, and bonding. It views other people as emotional, sensate beings like itself. It has sensory nerve connections to all the muscles and organs in the body, giving it exclusive access to the embodied sources of "gut" instincts. This is where those moments of insight (aha! moments) derive from when we are not intentionally focused on solving a problem. The right-brain also is the center of our emotional world. And, curiously, the right-brain operates subconsciously—completely below our conscious awareness.

On the other hand, the left-brain specializes in sophisticated cognitive and analytic skills. It sees everything mechanistically and reduces the world to schematics, diagrams, categories and lists. It needs order, coherence, and structure, and thus compartmentalizes all its knowledge. It sees everything in absolute, unambiguous black-or-white terms. In stark contrast to the right-brain, the left-brain is the neural center of our conscious self. Our left-brain 'thinks' very logically. Meet Mr. Spock from *Star Trek*! These characteristics are the source of our brilliant analytic, abstract thinking, allowing us to create marketing strategies, business action plans, and measurements for maintaining high-quality products.

Now we begin to get some sense of the radical differences in the realities of the left-brains and right-brains: the left-brain's world is goal-oriented, laser-focused, aggressive, unambiguous, and confident. The right-brain's world is broadly focused, taking in the gestalt, open to change, flexible to responses, considerate of possible options, and cautious. Having these two ways to view the world give us an extraordinary evolutionary edge—when they work in balance with each other. But they do not! Modern civilization has become highly biased in favor of the left-brain. Think about it for a moment; our left-brain is:

- conscious—it "thinks"
- verbal—it speaks!
- simplistic—it's uncomplicated!
- relatively unemotional—fewer messes!
- goal-oriented—gives us ambition and drive
- positive, optimistic, and confident (overly so!)
- coherent—makes logical sense of things.

Who *wouldn't* be attracted to these traits? In fact, some would consider this list as a model for exemplary business leadership! But two things are missing here: (1) a balance with the humane, people-centered right-brain, which is essential for building relationships that are inspiring and engaging—a critical factor for getting work accomplished; and (2) a darker side of our left-brain that we will explore further.

Research shows that our left-brain can operate with a chilling Machiavellian pragmatism. It sees the world and other people as objects to be manipulated and controlled. Moral values and ethics have no place in its vocabulary. It is self-centered and egotistical, evaluating and judging everyone and everything. It has limited sensory communication with the rest of the body; so it is literally "disembodied." It is also emotionally disconnected from other people. In effect, our left-brain is isolated in its own disembodied, self-referential, logical ivory tower, with no feelings of empathy, compassion, or social bonding. Do not forget that the evolutionary core of this part of our brain is focused on one thing only—finding and eating food for its survival, at any cost!

OUR ARROGANT LEFT-BRAIN

Let us look at one of the groundbreaking experiments that revealed just how our left-brain thinks with arrogant deception. Starting in the 1970s, Dr. Michael Gazzaniga and his colleagues in the United States worked with several patients who had the neural connections between their left and right hemispheres (the corpus callosum) surgically severed in order to reduce severe epileptic seizures. The bizarre results of the experiments conducted on "Joe" may sound stranger than fiction (cited in McGilchrist 2012).

Describing these experiments can be confusing, because the neural wiring from the two sides of the brain cross over and connect with the opposite sides of the body. For instance, Joe's *left*-brain is connected with his *right* eye and *right* hand. To minimize this confusion, I describe Joe's hands and eyes as left-brained or right-brained. Please focus while I explain this:

With the connecting nerves severed, the two halves of Joe's brain operate completely independently, with no communication or knowledge of what the other is thinking or doing. Joe's left hemisphere is the verbal part of his brain (like ours!); so when asked a question, it is his left-brain that responds verbally. Joe's right-brain can also hear the questions being asked, but can only respond nonverbally through physical movement of his right-brained hand.

The researchers simultaneously showed Joe two different pictures on a computer screen so that only his left-brained eye could see a chicken's foot, and his right-brained eye could see a snow scene. They then asked Joe to use his left-brained hand to pick a card from several placed in front of him that related to the chicken's foot, and he picked a photo of a chicken. Excellent! His left-brain is responding logically to the only object it is aware of—the chicken's foot. And then the researchers asked him to use his right-brained hand to also pick a card, and he chose a card with a

Figure 3.2.   Visual summary of what Joe sees and the cards he chooses.

snow shovel, which logically relates to the snow scene that he saw with his right-brain.

The researchers then asked Joe a trick question: "Why did you choose a snow shovel?" Now remember that by asking Joe to respond verbally he is relying on his left-brain to answer the question, and—here's the catch!— his left-brain had no knowledge of his right-brain seeing a snow scene or understanding why it chose a snow shovel. In other words, Joe's left-brain cannot *deny* what it has actually seen his right-brained hand do, but he cannot explain it either!

Rather than humbly acknowledging his inability to explain his actions, Joe confidently answered without hesitation: "I saw a claw and I picked a chicken, and you have to clean out the chicken shed with a shovel."

Using the chicken and chicken's foot as a reference (because that's what Joe actually *knows*), he quickly concocted a entirely fictional story about needing a shovel to clean out the chicken shed—even if it was a shovel designed for *snow*!

Here is the essence of this disturbing thinking process; the left-brain:

- draws *conclusions* of which it knows nothing about,
- is *certain* of its logic,

- *denies* any discrepancies in its logic, and
- *fabricates* a story to rationalize discrepancies.

In writing this chapter, I found it curious that no personal examples of my own came readily to mind. Nor have I witnessed many leaders be forthcoming in sharing their experiences. It seems we conveniently "forget" these episodes! We do not like our self-image to be threatened or embarrassed in front of others, especially at work. We have a tremendous need to defend our ego. If someone on the street would ask me for directions and I do not immediately know the answer, there is a critical voice inside me that immediately says something like, "You dummy, you should know this! Don't embarrass me with your stupidity. Say *something* so that you at least *appear* smart!" I then give the stranger directions I am not fully certain of, and everyone goes happily on their way. Not entirely: an unsettled voice inside me whispers, "Why did you do that?"

Looking back at the anagram game, this same kind of thinking process was at play. Does this type of disconnected logic and intense pressure to *look smart* sound familiar to any business meetings you might have been part of? Would you be willing to acknowledge that you have, in total self-confidence, acted out his scenario step by step?

The point of all this is *not* to embarrass me, you, or anyone else. The point is to name the unnamable—that we are not as logical or reasonable as we would like to think, and that our brain will lie to protect our self-image! This is an *inconvenient truth* about being human! It is part of how our brains operate! Yet the implications for business decisions being made every day in organizations all over the world are nothing less than profound.

ORGANIZATIONAL ARROGANCE

Chris Argyris, professor emeritus at Harvard Business School, coined the term *organizational defensive routines* to describe what we saw in Joe, except at an organizational level—creating a story we tell ourselves to cover up discrepancies in our logic (Argyris 1990). These collective thinking traps serve the same purpose—as a way for teams, departments, and organizations to avoid embarrassment or threat when things are not going as they should. One insidious characteristic of defensive routines is that they are denied when we are confronted with their existence. In other words, *the cover-up is covered up*!

One of the most dramatic examples of the consequences of organizational defensive routines is the disaster during the 1986 launch of the U.S. space shuttle *Challenger*. NASA prided itself on its ability to predict and avoid potentially fatal errors through flawless logic and reasoning. No astronaut had ever died after the moment of launch. But NASA had also recently experienced several embarrassing delays in getting the shuttle off the ground and felt political pressure to not delay any further. Hours before the planned launch, as temperatures fell below freezing at the Florida launch site, an engineer from a subcontracting company questioned the decision to go ahead with the launch when a certain rubber sealing ring on the fuel tanks had never been tested at sub-zero temperatures. In an emergency conference call, NASA's senior management called the engineer's loyalty, intelligence, and team spirit into question. When he could not show proof beyond doubt, the—fatal—decision to proceed with the launch was made. The seven astronauts aboard the *Challenger* died in a fiery explosion minutes after takeoff due to the failure of that sealing ring (Presidential Commission, 1986).

Our individual and collective thinking traps, especially when we are stressed or under pressure, can cause very intelligent people to make very stupid decisions. Remember that the left-brain is completely self-centered, literally perceives other people as objects, and has no moral values that would elicit feelings of guilt about telling a lie. It favors the positive, ego-centered emotions that result from winning and prevailing over others. It loves success and hates failure.

There are several other ways in which our minds can deceive us and cause us to think and act in ways we never intended. Let us explore three other *inconvenient truths* about our brains.

OUR MEMORY IS *NOT* PICTURE PERFECT

It is commonly believed that only older people with Alzheimer's disease or other forms of senility cannot accurately remember things from their past. In fact, *no one* accurately remembers their past, even though they may be *certain* that what they remember is as accurate as if they were looking at a photograph of it in their minds.

Scientists are finding that what we thought were fixed images of the past are more like digitally altered copies that has been "touched up" numerous times in a neural version of Photoshop. What we remember, whether it is 30 years ago or 3 days ago, has been modified by the experiences we have had in the meantime. Everything is exaggerated and colored, making our memories larger than life—either more pleasurable or more painful than they actually were.

This process is like the game of *telephone*, where a simple statement is whispered repeatedly around a circle only to find it has changed, often beyond recognition, by the end. This game is very amusing, yet something like this is happening in our brain *all* the time! A study conducted at Northwestern University in the United States showed how, every time students were asked to recall where they had placed an object on a grid, their accuracy decreased. They also found that every recall was more influenced by the previous recall (whether accurate or not) than the original action (Bridge, 2012).

Similar studies have shown that every time we pull a memory from our neural library, it is modified by our current or recent emotional state. The more intense the emotions were at the time of the event, the more inaccurate the "facts" of the memory become. This is why eye-witness testimony is now being questioned in the courts; a witness' accounting of the "facts" is nothing more than their own subjective *interpretation* of what happened. How often have we been in a business meeting and we hear team members argue over the facts—with multiple perspectives on the "truth"?

Again, we find the overconfident and arrogant certainty of our left-brain simply evading the reality of how the human mind actually operates. Our memory is *not* what we think. It is *not* an accurate record of past experience!

WE ARE *NOT* OBJECTIVE

Our brain's primary job is to quickly assess how threatening or safe any given experience might be for us and to then decide what action is needed. This is what potentially allows us to respond to circumstances more effectively and more quickly than any other living creature; this is a hard-wired survival strategy that keeps us at the top of the food chain.

But think about it. If we are evaluating our current experience based on our past experiences, which have been subjectively and emotionally stored in memory, how can we possibly be objective in evaluating our immediate experience? We are essentially filtering our experience through subjective memories of our past (or sometimes through idealized fantasies of the future!). Our accumulated assessments of what is safe or threatening—painful or pleasurable—have simply turned into a set of personal values or preferences—a very *subjective* view of the world, of what we like and do not like.

I like chocolate ice cream, but for me to proclaim that chocolate is *the* best ice cream flavor would be ridiculous and arrogant. It would be to confuse my subjective preferences with an objective truth. But this is how our left-brain works; it considers everything it thinks to be absolutely logical, coherent, and objective.

Most of us equate our thoughts—what we think—with what we believe we are. We take great pride of ownership in our thoughts, beliefs and points of view. As spiritual teacher Adyashanti puts it: "the mind shows up and says 'mine. That's mine. That's my thought.' ... Right at that point lies the genesis, the root, of all suffering and separation" (Adyashanti, 2004, p. 34). We begin to protect what we think is ours, and we can become quite defensive when someone else challenges our point of view. It becomes an existential threat because we take our thoughts to be who we are!

We pride ourselves on our perceived ability to perceive reality *objectively*. Yet we are all guilty of advocating our subjective preferences as if they embody the "truth" of reality. We—and every other business leader in the world—are making choices, taking decisions, and interacting with others based on our *subjective* biases. How aware are we of our thinking traps? How aware are we of our biases, judgments, and prejudices? How do they color our thoughts and interactions with work colleagues?

We also have the ability to manipulate data to justify a subjective point of view. Any finance person, if they speak candidly, will tell you that the numbers—"hard data"—can be interpreted in different ways. One of the fallacies of thinking in the business world is that metrics objectively drive decisions. But metrics merely measure; they are data points to help leaders make decisions. The reality of brain science conclusively says that human decision-making is driven by subjective emotions, not by data. Leaders seem to be able to deftly justify their decisions with data after having made an emotionally based decision! This is simply another variation of the *arrogantly right* thinking trap.

ANALYTICAL THINKING DOES *NOT* TRUMP INTUITION

Studies of the decision-making process of individuals like top fighter pilots and firefighters, who must make split-second decisions under extreme stress, find that they do not rely just on their cognitive, analytical left-brain skills but also on their subconscious, intuitive right-brain (Hoogendoorn, Merk, Roessingh, & Treur, 2009). They are more in touch with information coming in from their bodies, which are sensing the environment not with their thinking mind but through direct sensation. They make the "right" decision in a fraction of a second without consciously "thinking" about it.

Let us demystify the word *intuition*. Intuition is simply the way in which our right-brain processes information on a subconscious level; it processes information much faster than our left-brain. Intuition comes about by the integration of extremely swift sensory information coming from our body —the heart, the gut, the muscles, et cetera—with emotional processing occurring in our right-brain. An article by Matzler, Bailom, and Mooradian (2007) in *MIT Sloan Management Review* on intuitive decision-making says that when leaders use their intuition in their decision-making, they "bring into play a process in which knowledge, experience and emotions are linked." The article continues: "It is not a magical sixth sense or a paranormal process; nor does it signify either random and whimsical decision making or the opposite of reason" (p. 14).

It is unfortunate that the intuitive, right-brained means of processing information has been dismissively described as delusional, "not real," and untrustworthy. This is the voice of our mechanistic left-brain, which immediately dismisses anything that cannot be measured. But to dismiss the intuitive processing of our brain is simply a cognitive thinking trap.

The engineer who raised concerns about the sealing rings on the night before the launch of the doomed *Challenger* could not, in that moment, put his finger on the data to substantiate his concern. He was voicing his intuition—a *feeling* that things were not right. The NASA senior managers in their rational arrogance refused to take seriously the "gut" feeling of one of their experienced engineers—with disastrous consequences.

In this age of complex data overload, it is simply not possible for our left-brain's relatively slow, analytical thinking to absorb and utilize all information. Matzler et al. conclude their article on intuitive decision-making by saying that: "Analytics can never trump the intuition of a thoughtful executive, wrought by years of experience and accumulated knowledge, tempered by emotional intelligence" (Matzler, Bailon, & Todd, 2007, p. 15).

AN EXIT STRATEGY FROM OUR THINKING TRAPS: HUMBLE LEADERSHIP

Thinking traps are an inconvenient truth that most of us do not like to admit we have. This is especially true if you are a perfectionist, an over-achiever, ambitious, or a combination of all three. Organizations that pride themselves on being a culture of *high performance*, *excellence*, and a *can-do attitude* attract this employee type. In many organizations, acknowledging that you made a mistake—or even admitting that you *might* be wrong in your thinking—is considered a death knell. And this is when conditions are ripe for Argyris' (1990) defensive routines to show up on a large scale. The pressure to perform—when overly stressed—creates a culture of what Argyris calls skilled *incompetence*, because of the messes that ensue from the unrealistic expectations of being "perfect."

What is your definition of *perfect*? How do you know when you have achieved it? How does it drive your behavior in ways that in fact keep you from performing at your best? Can you admit that you have made a mistake—first to yourself and then to the stakeholders impacted by your actions?

I remember a chief executive officer describing how he had reluctantly agreed to receive professional coaching after receiving feedback from his boss about his arrogant leadership style. He proudly recalled how everything changed a few months later with his management team after the first time he admitted to everyone that he had actually made a mistake. He had incorrectly interpreted some financial data. But by taking the risk to be humble in front of them, his team's trust in him increased, and as a result it functioned much more effectively. This chief executive officer had learned that it was okay to be humble, and that acknowledging his imperfections would make him a more inspiring leader. Being comfortable and transparent with our cognitive imperfections is a leadership asset, not a liability. It makes us *human*. And *that* is inspiring.

We live in an very volatile, uncertain, complex, and ambiguous world. The acronym for these four words, VUCA, was coined by the U.S. military in the 1990s (Lawrence, 2014). It has also become a part of business lingo, especially after the 2008 financial meltdown. Our VUCA world requires a brave new leadership style.

The 2008 financial meltdown humbled GE's chief executive officer, Jeff Immelt, in ways he could never have imagined. He prided himself on his excellence in thinking and execution. But the unpredictable and uncontrollable events that unfolded in those weeks led him to understand that he could not possibly know or anticipate everything. After that personally humbling experience, Immelt began talking about humility as an essential leadership trait. It was added to GE's core values. How arrogant to believe that we—or anyone, for that matter—have the ability to accurately see or anticipate everything.

Neuroscience shows that our left-brain can lie, that it possesses an arrogance that is certain of its conclusions and of the accuracy of its memory, that is certain of its objectivity, and rejects any intuitive feelings.

The good news is that these thinking traps can be managed with self-awareness and a courageous commitment to be a humble leader.

One of the most brilliant minds of our time, Dr. Richard Feynman—theoretical physicist, renowned educator, and Nobel laureate—sums up his approach to science and to life thus: "I can live with doubt and uncertainty. I think it's much more interesting than to live with answers which might be wrong. I have approximate answers and different degrees of certainty about various things, but I'm not absolutely certain of anything" (Feyman, 1981). Do we dare to be among the humble, brilliant leaders such as Dr. Feynman?

A LEADERSHIP PRACTICE: HUMILITY

Think of the arguments you have been involved in during business meetings when you and others have been—with equal and absolute certainty—"right." A simple leadership practice is to preface almost everything you say with a qualifier such as, "This is my understanding of ..." or "I might be mistaken, but I believe ..." When we start asking questions like *What am I not seeing about this issue?*, we help create a culture that avoids certainty and nurtures a culture of curiosity and humility, a culture that encourages the full creative potential of our minds.

REFERENCES

Adyashanti. (2004). *Emptiness dancing*. Boulder, CO: Sounds True.

Argyris, C. (1990). *Overcoming organizational defenses: Facilitating organizational learning*. Boston, MA: Allyn & Bacon.

Bridge, D., & Paller, K. (2012). Neural correlates of reactivation and retrieval-induced distortion. *Journal of Neuroscience, 32*(35), 12144–12151.

Feynman, R. (1981, November 23). Excerpted from BBC Television program *Horizon: Feynman, The pleasure of finding things out*. Series 18, Episode 9.

Hoogendoorn, M., Merk, R., Roessingh, J., & Treur, J. (2009). Modelling a fighter pilot's intuition in decision making on the basis of Damasio's somatic marker hypothesis. In *Proceedings of the 17th Congress of the International Ergonomics Association, IEA'09* (pp. 279–280).

Kahneman, D. (2013). *Thinking, fast and slow*. New York, NY: Farrar, Straus and Giroux.

Lawrence, K. (2014). *Developing leaders in a VUCA environment* (UNC Executive Development Newsletter). Chapel Hill, NC: University of North Carolina Kenan-Flagler Business School.

Matzler, K., Bailon, F., & Todd, M. A. (2007). Intuitive decision making. *MIT Sloan Management Review, 49*(1), 13–15.

McGilchrist, I. (2012). *The master and his emissary: The divided brain and the making of the Western world*. New Haven, CT: Yale University Press.

Presidential Commission: On the Space Shuttle Challenger Accident. (1986, June 5). Washington, DC: Government Printing Office.

Taleb, N. (2005). *Fooled by randomness*. New York, NY: Random House.

Taleb, N. (2010). *The black swan: The impact of the highly improbable*. New York, NY: Random House.

CHAPTER 4

THE MINDFUL LEADER

Focusing Your Attention on What Matters

Jim Shipley

One evening, an old Cherokee man told his grandson about a battle that goes on inside people. He said, "The battle is between the two wolves that live in all of us.

"One is anger, envy, jealousy, sorrow, regret, greed, arrogance, self-pity, guilt, resentment, inferiority, lies, false pride, superiority, and ego.

"The other is joy, peace, love, hope, serenity, humility, kindness, benevolence, empathy, generosity, truth, compassion, and faith."

The youngster thought about it for a minute and then asked: "Which wolf wins?"

The old man simply replied, "The one you feed."

OBJECTIVE

Our brains have a limited capacity to focus attention. As leaders we need to be aware that our brains have a tendency to focus attention in habitual, unconstructive ways.

Advanced Leadership Insights: How to Lead People and Organizations to Ultimate Success
pp. 37–49
Copyright © 2017 by Information Age Publishing
All rights of reproduction in any form reserved.

However, we can develop the ability to manage our focus of attention through self-awareness as well as mental and emotional discipline. Several leadership practices can help us build self-awareness and discipline.

Is Your Attention Focused on What Matters Most?

I often hear leaders describing themselves as frantic doers—driven by what the company wants, by what their boss wants, by the meetings listed in their agendas, by constant fire-fighting, and by distractions that invade every moment of their workday. Then there are the demands of their families and spouses. They are like hamsters on a wheel that never stops! Are you a frantic doer, or is your attention focused on what matters most?

How do we move from being a frantic doer to being an inspiring leader? As challenging as it may be, a critical success factor for every leader is to *consistently focus one's attention and energy on what matters most* and to avoid the ever-present trap of distractions that surround us. How we focus our attention is at the core of our—cognitive, emotional, and social-intelligence. It is about self-awareness and self-discipline. It is about which wolf we choose to feed.

To enhance our self-awareness and to develop a more disciplined focus of attention, we must first understand exactly how our brain manages our attention and especially what its limitations are. We tend to believe that our brain has an unlimited ability to focus its attention and is highly agile in managing where it focuses. It is neither! look at some discoveries about the challenges to our brains in order to focus our attention.

LIMITATIONS OF OUR BRAINS

On average, we can only remember five to seven numbers if asked to recall a list of numbers. There is a very small area in the executive functioning region of our brains that is devoted to our focus of attention. This elite neural real estate is commonly referred to as our *working memory*—the space where we temporarily hold concepts in our mind while we actively think about them. David Rock, in *Your Brain at Work*, likens this space to the stage of a very small theater on which only a few actors can comfortably perform at the same time (Rock, 2009). Our job, as the stage manager, is to optimize the limited space for working memory.

A common misunderstanding about our working memory theater is that we can have several plays on at the same time—in other words, that we can multitask. The brain science is unequivocal: *We cannot multitask!* We cannot focus our attention in a concerted way on more than one thing at a time. I will repeat this, in case you were checking your messages while trying to read this paragraph: *We cannot multitask!* However, we can perform multiple tasks that require little or no effort—for instance, when on a conference call and also responding to e-mails. Let us face it: we are not doing either task particularly well! What is insidious is that we tend to consistently overestimate our mental capacities (Kahneman, 2013). We actually think we *can* multitask and that we can do it well! This is one limitation of our brains we must to come to terms with if we expect to realistically master our focus of attention to maximize our leadership performance.

Cognitive thinking consumes a tremendous amount of oxygen and glucose. We cannot sustain a state of focused attention for very long, typically not more than an hour or so. Switching our focus of attention from one idea to another also requires a great deal of energy; it can take upwards of 20 minutes for our mind to settle completely into a new focus.

So our brain has devised an interesting strategy to minimize energy consumption while maximizing brain function: *It is lazy! Very lazy!* It relies on its ability to effortlessly repeat activities it has already learned. In other words, our brains love ruts—habitual behavior—even if such behavior is not focused on what matters most!

We work on autopilot all the time. For instance, we drive almost entirely automatically. Are we aware of when we are operating on autopilot in our leadership roles? Are we making a conscious choice or slipping into unconscious habits? Have we stopped to reflect how we might be stuck in ways that are reinforcing behaviors that we do not want?

Compulsive or addictive behavior is the most extreme form; *everyone* indulges in it in one way or another. For instance, are you a workaholic? Or do you constantly check your communication device even when you know there are no new messages? When we are under stress, we are even more inclined to revert to addictive, compulsive behaviors in a desperate attempt to soothe our agitated inner state. We know it does not work, but we do it anyway. Stress takes energy away from our brain's executive functions and wreaks havoc with our ability to stay focused. We are more likely to focus on all the negatives rather than the positives, and are also more vulnerable to distractions.

For a long time, I had the habit to read the newspaper early in the morning to find out what was happening in the world. One day, in a moment of insight, I realized that almost always after reading the news, I felt agitated and frustrated, even angry. I also felt powerless to do anything about what I was reading. And this was how I started my day! Which wolf was I feeding?

I could easily rationalize reading the news by pointing out that it was important for my work. But did I really need to do it early in the morning, when I was barely awake and emotionally not ready for horrific stories? I was following a habit I had fallen into.

So I canceled my newspaper subscription (this was before the days of electronic devices!). It was not an easy decision, because I could feel how addicted I was to reading the news—including the bad news! In psychology, this is called *negative merging*, and it is a powerful way of distraction from focusing on what matters. Worse still: negative merging is contagious! We love to negatively merge with others in their bad news. When someone arrives late for a meeting and blames traffic for their delay, others will start to talk about how terrible the traffic is, how it has gotten worse in the past few years, perhaps offering their own personal negative story. This is a classic case of a group of people feeding the wrong wolf. How does this show up in your team or among colleagues? It is *much* more prevalent than we realize.

What We Focus on Changes Our Brains

Neuroscientists have found that conscious awareness—where we focus our attention—literally changes the synaptic connections between neurons in our brains. Studies on London taxi drivers show that the area of their brain involved in geographic location is physically larger than control groups. The same is true of virtuoso violinists, whose brain area associated with motor dexterity for the fingers of their left hand is significantly enlarged.

On the other hand, when we stop focusing on something, the number of synaptic connections will decrease over time. This is called *pruning*, and it seems to be a natural and necessary part of the development of the brain. Recent research indicates that autistic patients have less pruning in certain critical parts of their brains, causing their neural networks to be over-active. This would explain why they are characteristically overreactive in certain social situations and more prone to epileptic seizures (Belluck, 2014).

Where we focus our attention reinforces neural circuits that cause our mind to focus on that same thought in the future. In the two wolves analogy, we are likely to feed the same wolf in the future that we have fed in the past. This happens whether or not we are *conscious* of which wolf we are feeding. Our focus changes our brain even when we are not aware of it! This is why self-awareness is such a critical skills set to master—it is the key to giving ourselves more choice in how we operate in the world.

Limitations of Our Brain

- Our brain cannot multitask.
- Disruptions and distractions drain our brain of energy and intelligence.

- Our brain is lazy, compulsive, and addictive—it loves habitual behavior.
- Our brain is attracted to negative thoughts.
- What we focus on teaches our brain to prefer that focus in the future.
- Our brain is either task-focused or *gestalt*-focused, and cannot do both at once.

Two Types of Attention

A popular YouTube video originating from a study on human attention shows two teams each passing a basketball. The viewer is asked to count the number of times a particular team passes the ball.

Because our brain has been tasked to track something very specific, we are probably very accurate in our assessments of the number of passes. But then the video is shown again, and we are asked to see if there was anything we missed the first time around.

We are now focusing broadly on everything in the clip. In plain sight, someone in a gorilla costume walks casually into the middle of the two teams, beats its chest, and then walks off. Most people simply cannot believe they did not see the gorilla the first time around. Yet, according to brain science, this is very predictable because different networks in our brain are being activated.

Scientists call these two attention networks *task-positive* and *task-negative*. There seems to be a close association between *task-positive* and our left-brain's laser-focused attention, and between *task-negative* and our right-brain's *gestalt*-focused attention (see Chapter 4 of this book).

When we think about improving our focus, we probably think about how we can increase the task-focused side of our brain. This is where most of us try to operate most of the time. Our society values task-focusedness. And company leaders are constantly reminded to "stay focused on the task."

But what are leaders' tasks? Much of it about seeing the big picture, laying out a vision, goals, and strategy. This requires a different kind of thinking than counting the number of ball passes! It requires seeing the *gestalt*; it requires the task-negative brain network.

Unfortunately, this network has become identified with an unproductive, daydreaming mind. Yet, it is this wandering mind that allows us to see the big picture and to see the blinding flash of the obvious—like the gorilla. It is in this wandering mode where we have insights and *eureka* moments, like Archimedes had one day while stepping into the bath.

The chief executive officer of a bank described his *eureka* moment about the loans the bank was offering one day while shopping. The bank had placed a limit on personal loans based on rigorous risk analysis. But as the chief executive officer's wandering mind noticed the price of tires in a store window, he realized that the bank's loans would allow a customer to buy one or two new tires for their car, but not a set of four! The bank's limit was appropriate to its risk standards, but totally impractical in terms of how customers could use it. As a result, the bank increased its loan limit by a small margin, and its loan business increased!

Visionary thinking, strategic focus, creativity, innovation, out-of-the-box thinking—all these insights arise from the wandering mind. If companies are *truly* interested in promoting these values, they will find ways to reward their leaders for "wandering mind time!" Google is an example of a company that encourages task-negative thinking.

Developing our focus is about consciously deciding which attention type is needed at any given moment. Researchers have found that it is our insula, a small structure deep in the center of our brain, that seems to be the central switching mechanism for these two attention modes (Levitin, 2014). The insula is also intimately involved in regulating our emotional state. Thus, it plays a crucial role in coordinating our focus of attention with body awareness and action, along with the regulation of emotions. Refining the insula's coordinating function appears to give world-class athletes the Olympic-winning edge through the precise use of their energy and focus (Upson, 2012), especially under extreme physical and emotional stress. Even though the insula is not in our conscious awareness, we nonetheless have the ability to influence it, especially through mind-disciplining techniques called *mindfulness*. This same fine-tuning of the insula can also support exemplary leadership.

Now that we have a better understanding of the challenges to our brain concerning focusing, let us look at some of the distractions that are common and habitual in many leaders. Which of these hold true for you?

COMMON DISTRACTIONS FOR LEADERS

Addiction to Your Communication Device

Your communication device is an *addiction* device! Are you addicted? Are you constantly allowing it to interrupt what you are doing? Do you take it home with you after work? Do you take it to bed with you at night and leave it on while you're asleep? Do you respond to messages in the middle of the night? I have had leaders confess to all of the above! Which wolf are you feeding?

We are overloaded by information and stimuli. Attention deficit disorder may be partially genetic, but the fast-paced, chaotic world we live in is fertile ground for challenges to stay focused on what matters.

A study at the University of London several years ago bombarded smart business professionals with e-mails and text messages. Their IQs were measured and compared to their IQs prior to the test. Women had lost 5 points and men 15. Constantly checking your smartphone literally makes you dumber!

I am encouraged when I hear testimonials from leaders who say they now turn off their cellphone on weekends or have no longer respond to messages after a certain time in the evening—*and* none of these leaders have been fired or even reprimanded for setting sensible boundaries. They say their performance is better than when they had no boundaries. They can now devote more of their attention to what really matters at a given moment—responding to important messages, getting a good night's sleep, or playing attentively with their children.

Focus on Tasks and Goals at the Expense of People

The primary goal of every business is to make money. Businesses do this by setting and achieving goals. This is a necessary part of business. However, leaders often lose sight of the fact that it is people who execute these goals. If we become obsessed with one at the expense of the other, we risk losing the core of a sustainable business enterprise. I know of very few organizations who have the problem of being overly focused on the people side of the business. I know a great many organizations that constantly risk having a disengaged, uninspired workforce, because they are obsessed with meeting their numbers.

Neuroscientists have discovered a fascinating and relevant element of the brain: When we are not focused on a task (task-negative attention), such as counting the number of ball passes, our brain naturally defaults to focusing on yourself and other people. This so-called *default system* resides primarily in the brain structures associated with being social. Interestingly, this socially oriented system goes quiet when we focus on doing a task. We pay attention to the ball being passed, rather than the people passing the ball. In other words, we cannot simultaneously split our attention between a task and people. Thus, we must be especially vigilant concerning balancing our focus on people as we do things.

Finding a balance between a task and people is not easy! First, the organizational culture may push you toward a task emphasis. But what are your personal biases? Do we have a prefer tasks over people? If so, we must bear in mind that much of our job is about inspiring others to get a task done and performing at their best rather than doing the work ourselves!

Focus on What Is Wrong Rather Than What Is Right

A company that "strives for perfection" or "aspires to the highest quality standards" or that "demands excellence" also has a shadow side: there is a tendency to be obsessed with what is wrong or what is imperfect, at the expense of acknowledging the great things that people are doing daily. In the age of striving for six-sigma quality, it is all too easy to focus on all the defects, not only in the production line, but also in people.

People need positive reinforcement, and regularly. How many times in the past week have you acknowledged a team member for the good work they're doing? If not, why not? Which beliefs about yourself and others drives your focus only on what is not working rather than on what is working well? An inspiring leader is not just a taskmaster, but also someone who demonstrates in words their belief in the goodness of people. It is possible to strive for perfection *and* to acknowledge the great work that is being done along the way.

Dr. John Gottman, a clinical psychologist, has spent most of his career looking at what makes a couple's relationship healthy (Gottman & Silver, 2015). He has identified a magic ratio: 5 to 1. If there are at least five positive interactions to every one negative one, the relationship is likely to remain stable. He has proven this by accurately predicting 90% of the time whether a couple will divorce within 10 years based on observing one conversation between them!

Just one negative interaction—a judgmental look, a demeaning tone of voice, nonconstructive feedback, or an outright argument, yelling, or a fight—can cause lasting damage to a relationship. Gottman's (2015) research shows that five positive interactions are needed to neutralize one negative interaction. This principle for successful intimate relationships can also be applied to business relationships. How are your conversations with team members? Do you achieve the 5:1 ratio, or will your employees get "divorced" from you?

Are You Doing Other People's Work

Most leaders who describe themselves as frantic doers also spend 30%, 50%, or even 75% of their time doing others' work. They do things that are not in their job description and that others are accountable for. Yet the frantic doer seems to have enough time to take on such additional tasks.

This is compulsive behavior. The first question is: *Why do you do it?* You might say that you do not trust others to get the work done, or that others cannot do it as well or as swiftly. You step in because you feel rewarded by it: you feel important, you feel indispensable, you feel liked, and/or you feel appreciated. Your boss may think you're a hard worker. Your team has become disempowered and dependent on you. Your family wonders why you're not home. And you are up until late at night—doing other's work!

Where is your focus? Is it on what matters? Do you make time for your aspirations when you're drowning in other's work? Why are you not focused on coaching and on developing your team's capacities? Why are you not setting boundaries for yourself? You likely have some beliefs about yourself and others that disempower you and them. If this is true, then serious and sober conversations are in order with your spouse, your children, your team, and your boss. This must be explored and corrected if you are to focus on what matters.

Are You Leading, Managing, or Coaching?

Most leaders today have responsibilities relating to managing, leading, and coaching—among others. Although the words are often used interchangeably, they describe very different responsibilities:

- *Leaders* inspire others to do their best. They set a vision. They are strategic.
- *Managers* get the results. They manage resources, people, and time. They are tactical.
- *Coaches* help to develop others. They empower others by "teaching them how to fish, rather than giving them fish."

Each of these responsibilities require a different mindset, different skills, and a different *attention focus. What drives your focus? Have you fallen into habitual work patterns from the past that may well no longer be appropriate? Are you allocating the necessary time to each job so that you and your team are successful?*

Let us do a reality check: Think about your average work day. How much time do you spend leading, managing, coaching, and doing others' work? Write down a percentage next to each of these four roles, so they total 100%. *Why is your attention focused in this way? Do these numbers reflect where your attention should be?* Repeat the exercise; this time, write down the percentages you feel would better reflect an appropriate focus on what matters most in your particular job. *What do you need to do to make these percentages reflect the reality of your focus?*

Are You Playing the Victim?

We like to blame our problems on other people or on circumstances. We quickly focus our attention on anything we can point to.

I had just landed in Amsterdam after a sleepless 11-hour night flight from San Francisco. I was in a bad mood and still had an 1.5-hour train trip home. As I stood waiting for the train, I heard an announcement informing us that the train has been canceled. I exploded. My focus immediately went to the Dutch train system. "They are *never* on time! They are *always* unreliable." And I made it personal; they had done this to me! I felt totally justified to be righteously angry at this injustice! I was a victim of the Dutch train system. *And* I was focusing on something I could do absolutely nothing about—a canceled train.

After a few painful moments of rage, I realized what I was doing. I stopped and asked myself: "Jim, what do you want right now?" The answer was immediate and clear: "I just want to get home." With this question, I began reframing my story, from being a victim of the Dutch train system to being compassionate with myself, recognizing that I was tired and irritable, and I took responsibility for what I needed to do to get home.

Some Dutch trains are canceled; most trains run on time. That is the way it is. And sometimes it happens at inopportune moments. We make things personal and feel affronted when things do not go how we think they should. Victimhood renders us powerless and unable to respond to what is happening in our lives. My attention was feeding the wrong wolf, and my outburst did *nothing* to help me figure out the quickest way to get home.

Feeding the negative wolf can be seductive and can feel satisfying in a righteous way. It is a form of negative merging. *But what is it giving me? What do I really want? What matters to me in that moment? Do I want to be right, angry, and stuck on the platform? Or do I want to take whatever action I need in order to get home?* It is my choice …

It is *not* what happens to us in our lives that really matters—pleasant and difficult circumstances are part of being human. What *really* matters is how we *respond* to what happens in our lives. Like me on that platform, you may not have a choice about your circumstances, but we *always* have a choice about how we *respond* to them (Kofman, 2006). This is where our focus should be.

Being a leader in any company is fertile ground for victimhood. It is very easy to feel powerless at the hands of top management, the matrix organization, functional silos, and corporate politics. You may feel righteous in your indignation, but *where does it get you? Which wolf are you feeding?* These organizational issues are the reality of your world at work.

These are your circumstances. *Where is your focus? And where does it need to be for you to get your work done?*

When you are playing Poker, you have no control over which cards you get. Sometimes you get great cards, and sometimes not. If you get a bad hand, and you immediately think, "This is a lousy hand; I can't win this game," you have just declared yourself a victim of the cards you were dealt. In poker, even when you have a really bad hand, you can sometimes still win. So rather than focusing on what you cannot change, focus on how you can best play this hand.

The same is true when you get a good hand. When you think, "This is a great hand; I cannot lose," you are also declaring yourself a victim, because you're focused on the cards and not how you are going to play them. You have closed the options at your disposal by making such a declaration of confidence.

The reality with poker, as with most things in life, is that you will win some games and you will lose some. If you focus on whether you are winning or losing, you are focusing on what you cannot control. It is guaranteed that you will suffer, because you never win as much as you want.

Here is the radical attention shift: rather than focusing on whether you win or lose, focus on playing the game to the best of your ability. When the game is over, regardless whether you have won or lost, you can walk away satisfied, knowing that you played it to the best of your ability. It feels great when you win, and not so good when you lose. But with this attention shift, on how we *respond* to what life presents us with, we are able to handle life's ups and downs much better.

I witnessed a devastated sales manager in Singapore a few years ago as she shared the life-shattering experience of not reaching her sales goals during the last quarter, for the first time ever in her career! She had lost the game, *but it was not a game to her.* She had failed in her eyes; to her, it felt like a matter of life and death. It did not matter that there were factors beyond her control that made it impossible for her to reach her goals. She was a victim of her own doing. It was clear that she had played the best she could with the cards she had been dealt. But her strong competence as a sales manager no longer mattered—she had failed, and that was what mattered to her.

Nowadays, business goals are almost a religious matter. I have seen too many leaders like this one who think that their sole focus should be to reach their numbers. And I consistently see leaders suffering emotionally because they are unable to say to themselves, "I played the hand I was dealt to the best of my ability. It is unfortunate that I didn't reach my target."

We cannot avoid being a victim; this is unrealistic. We will always have situations when we unwittingly step into the victim role. But we can learn to recognize these moments and get out of them more swiftly. We can move from being victims of our circumstances to being masters of our fate.

CONCLUSION

Even though our brains have a limited capacity to focus our attention, it can also be trained to supports us to more consistently focus on what we want rather than being a victim to all the distractions we face daily. This leadership practice is at the heart of emotional intelligence—one that is much more important than IQ in distinguishing exemplary leaders (Goleman, 1995, 2013).

Developing the discipline to remain focused on what matters is not easy, but it is possible to improve with sustained self-awareness and practice. It is a worthy endeavor to support ourselves in moving from being a frantic doer to being an inspiring leader, and in choosing which wolf in ourselves we feed.

Leadership Practices: Structuring Our Time and Energy to Focus Our Attention

- *Prioritize daily actions*: Do this when you are most alert, because it is one of the most energy-intensive thought processes your brain will perform.
- *Create a to-do list*: Holding your action plan in our mind reduces the capacity of your limited working memory; writing it down frees your mind to think more optimally.
- *Block your day into project periods*: Limit your e-mail management to specific periods daily rather than constant interruptions all day long.
- *Schedule your most thought-intensive activities when you are most alert*: Work with your natural energy cycle. For instance, many people are most alert in the morning; to clear your in-box then is not optimal to your energy cycle.
- *Turn off those message notification pings*: This is a built-in distraction system with no practical use!
- *Take regular breaks*: Your brain needs a rest every hour or so.
- *Set clear boundaries about interruptions*: Quickly determine whether an interruption warrants your immediate attention or whether it needs to be respectfully deferred to a more appropriate time. People appreciate respectful clarity.

- *Appropriately delegate tasks*: Do this in a way that builds mutual trust and confidence, and insures successful task fulfillment.
- *Keep your meetings focused and productive*: Use your meeting facilitation skills to create and maintain a group's focus. Virtual meetings require vigilant attention to keep a group focused.

REFERENCES

Belluck, P. (2014, August 21). Study finds that brains with autism fail to trim synapses as they develop. *The New York Times*. Retrieved from http://www.nytimes.com/2014/08/22/health/brains-of-autistic-children-have-too-many-synapses-study-suggests.html

Goleman, D. (1995). *Emotional intelligence*. New York, NY: Bantam Books.

Goleman, D. (2013, December). The focused leader. *Harvard Business Review*. Retrieved from https://hbr.org/2013/12/the-focused-leader

Gottman, J. M., & Silver, N. (2015). *The seven principles for making marriage work* (2nd edition). New York, NY: Harmony Books.

Kahneman, D. (2013). *Thinking, fast and slow* (1st ed). New York, NY: Farrar, Straus and Giroux.

Kofman, F. (2006). *Conscious business: How to build value through values*. Boulder, CO: Sounds True.

Levitin, D. J. (2014, August 9). Hit the reset button in your brain. *New York Times*. Retrieved from http://www.nytimes.com/2014/08/10/opinion/sunday/hit-the-reset-button-in-your-brain.html

Rock, D. (2009). *Your brain at work: Strategies for overcoming distraction, regaining focus, and working smarter all day long* (1st ed). New York, NY: Harper Business.

Upson, S. (2012, July 24). A single brain structure may give winners that extra physical edge. *Scientific American*. Retrieved from http://www.scientificamerican.com/article/olympics-insula-gives-edge/

PART II

LEADING OTHERS TO ULTIMATE SUCCESS

CHAPTER 5

THE FIVE SUCCESS FACTORS OF A TRULY HIGH-PERFORMING TEAM

Katja Kruckeberg

"The whole is greater than the sum of its parts"

—Aristotle

OBJECTIVE

In this chapter, I explain the five success factors of high-performing teams. My guidance and insights for leaders are aimed at building the team they need to achieve the results they strive for. While these five factors are based on solid research, I take a practical approach to team development.

THE EMERGENCE OF TEAMWORK

The widespread employment of teams has become indispensable to successfully operating organizations across industries throughout the world.

Advanced Leadership Insights: How to Lead People and Organizations to Ultimate Success
pp. 53–9

Organizations establish teams to tackle challenges that are too comprehensive for individual employees to complete on their own. When, for instance, a new product needs to be launched, people from all parts of an organization are drawn together in cross-functional teams to combine their expertise and experience to jointly work toward this goal. The increased globalization of work has also contributed to the emergence of teamwork worldwide (Boundless, 2016). Many of the challenges global companies face need to be addressed "glocally," thus considering the connections between global and local businesses. To do so, companies often form virtual teams, which enable large organizations to employ the knowledge, experience, and skills of people regardless of where they are located. These relatively new team types all benefit from new IT and telecommunications technologies. There is also an increasing use of project teams, which are formed for a specific time to work toward a larger goal. Project team members often belong to different functional groups and are chosen for the specific skills set they offer the team. In short, it is common for an organization to have many team types across the organization.

THE POTENTIAL BENEFITS OF TEAMWORK

The potential advantages of teamwork are based on several factors, each accounting for different aspects of the overall benefit of teamwork:

1. **Higher-quality outcomes**: Teamwork creates outcomes that make better use of resources and produce richer ideas.
2. **Innovation**: Individuals who combine their knowledge, expertise, and experience create more innovative ideas than individuals on their own.
3. **Higher efficiency**: Since teams combine the efforts of many individuals, they can accomplish more in less time than an individual working alone.
4. **Greater effectiveness**: When people coordinate their efforts, they can divide up roles and can deploy their strengths to achieve better business results.
5. **Collective learning and motivation**: The social aspect of teamwork provides a superior work experience for team members, which can lead to higher motivation. People learn from one another, push one another to accelerate their learning, and celebrate successes together (Boundless, 2016).

INEFFECTIVE TEAMWORK

Reading through these potential benefits of teamwork should delight every manager. But reflect for a moment on your own experiences with teamwork: *Do teams always create synergetic effects by working together? Does Aristotle's notion that the whole is greater then the sum of its parts really apply the moment a group of talented people form a team?*

Common sense and recent research call the benefits of teamwork into question. J. Richard Hackman, Professor of Social and Organizational Psychology at Harvard University and a leading expert on team performance in business, has spent several decades investigating and questioning the wisdom of teams. His research shows that people are not always good at teamwork and that many teams perform less well than individuals working in parallel, despite all their extra resources. "When you have a team, the possibility exists that it will generate magic, producing something extraordinary, a collective creation of previously unimagined quality or beauty. But don't count on it" (Hackman, as cited in Coutu, 2009).

SUCCESS FACTORS THAT LEAD TO HIGH PERFORMANCE

The key questions are therefore: *What does it take to form a high-performing team? What are the success factors and what are the typical pitfalls a manager needs to watch out for when forming a new team and managing an existing one over time?*

I present a model, a diagnostic tool, and exercises to help leaders take a thoughtful, yet simple, approach to building and managing their high-performing team. This model—*The Five Success Factors of a High-performing Team*—(Figure 5.1) is based on more then 15 years of hands-on experience and research by my team and me, as well as on state-of-the-art knowledge and research results from the leading people and organizations researching high performance, leadership, and human behavior in teams around the globe.

This is not the first model to seek to explain peak performance in teams. So, why bother? The answer is that, in my many years of leadership consulting, I have not come across a model that truly works in practice. They may all have some academic appeal, but when applied in practice, the teams I worked with struggled to make sense of them. Important aspects of teamwork were missing. Therefore, I fine-tuned my thinking over the decade (the model, the practical activities, and the diagnostic tool) and tested it with the teams I worked with. *The Five Success Factors of a High-performing Team* pyramid is the result of all these efforts. We will now explore it in some depth.

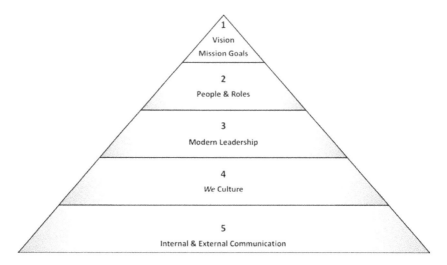

Figure 5.1.   The five success factors of a high-performing team.

Success Factor 1: Team Vision, Goals, and Mission

A team is a group of people who work together toward a common goal. This is the most basic definition of a team. Sharing a set of team goals (and, ideally, a shared vision) is the first reason to form a team; it is a team's reason for existing. However, in practice, we often see that this set of shared team goals is either missing, or the team members are not aware of them.

Professor Hackman's research shows that team members (here, executive teams of leading organizations from around the world!) often have little or no clarity regarding their team goals. These teams lack the most basic prerequisite of successful teamwork: A shared understanding of the team's reason for existing, which means that they cannot achieve peak performance.

All high-performing teams I have worked with have a shared understanding about their future direction. They thus continuously invest time in maintaining and building on this understanding in an ever-changing business environment, as this is the only way to create synergies together. These teams have agreed on *what* they want to achieve together, written down in the form of a vision statement with shared goals and individual ones. Similarly, they have also agreed on *how* they want to work together in order to be successful, written down in the form of a mission or team brand statement. I will now explain team vision, team goals, and team mission in some detail.

Team Vision

Creating a team vision statement is about describing your team's desired future. You are setting the direction toward which you are heading. It is not so much about how you are going to get there, but about defining the destination you are striving toward. The team vision statement is ambitious, dynamic, and will hopefully inspire your team to perform to the best of their abilities.

A team vision statement:

- describes the team's destination
- sets the team's purpose
- is easy to comprehend
- inspires enthusiasm
- creates commitment
- bridges the present and the future.

Organizational vision statements are created at the top of the organization. However, achieving the organizational vision can only happen with a buy-in by the entire organization, which consists of multiple high-performing teams pursuing excellence in their own right.

Team Goals

Besides clearly defined goals for the individuals working in the team, the team needs a clearly defined and communicated set of team goals. Ideally, these goals have been agreed upon together to ensure high levels of awareness and commitment toward these goals. A product team goal could be determining the short-term and long-term profit targets for its new and old products. Product team managers may aim to increase the annual profits by X% for the most popular product and Y% for older models. Whatever the case, team goals should be SMART (Specific, Measurable, Attainable, Realistic, and Timely). It might therefore be unrealistic for a team to aim to increase the annual profits by 100% in a highly competitive marketplace. The goals should therefore reflect the context in which the team operates.

Team Mission

A team vision statement describes the destination your team is working toward. When you create your team mission statement (ideally with your team), you are defining *how* you will get there. The advantage of agreeing on a mission statement is that it offers a frame of reference for daily behaviors that create the conditions for success. Success with ultimately achieving your team goals can usually not be guaranteed 100%. Many internal and external factors interfere with the business results a team or an organization achieves. However, how we behave daily can mostly be planned and controlled.

The Leader's Role

The biggest pitfall leaders should look out for in their team is individuals who focus only on their individual roles and on their assigned tasks at the expense of teamwork. Under pressure, people tend to focus on their own goals and might not equally care if and how they contribute to the overall team goals. It is the leader's responsibility to ensure that the team members also focus on the team's vision, goals, and mission by taking time collectively to discuss progress concerning the team vision, goals, and mission, as well as by ensuring that rewards are based on both individual and collective achievements.

GERMANY'S NATIONAL FOOTBALL TEAM

Sports teams are a good example of how teams work. Since I have extensively worked with and researched high-performance teams in professional football, I share relevant results from this research. An example of how a team vision and mission can be brought to life and can help a team to succeed is Germany's national football team under the leadership of Jürgen Klinsmann between 2004 and 2006, when the World Championship took place in Germany. When Klinsmann accepted the position of coach, Germany regarded the team very negatively. The country had not been successful for a number of years, and its football was known to be functional but boring to watch (a perception also held outside Germany).

When Klinsmann took over, he was determined to lead the team to success, to win the World Championship (vision) and to revolutionize both German football (mission) and the infrastructure behind it. As Oliver Bierhoff, who was part of the management team, put it: "Our vision was to win the world championship. However, we wanted to play a new kind of dynamic football, take risks and entertain the audience. We wanted to inspire all the children in Germany to play football again. We wanted to win as a team and act as ambassadors of our country." Although the German team did not become world champions in 2006, they were seen as extremely successful, coming in third, playing exciting and dynamic football, celebrating like world champions and helping Germany as a country to improve its reputation abroad. They also laid the foundation for the development of Germany's national team in the following years, which ultimately led to its winning the World Championship in 2014. In business, as in sports, this kind of success cannot ultimately be planned. However, creating the conditions for success makes winning and peak performance most likely.

Success Factor 2: People and Roles

The second success factor of a high-performing team has to do with the people on the team. A team leader should find a way to first decide who is on the team, who takes which role, and who is responsible for which task. Let us start with the first: Who is on the team?

Who Is on the Team

Depending on the situation in which the team leader operates, he or she usually finds a mix of two possibilities: either (as often the case in project teams) the team leader has the opportunity to build a new team from scratch, or (as is mostly the case) a promoted leader takes over an existing team.

Forming a New Team

If the team leader has the opportunity to build a new team, it is important to get the right people on board: People who have the skills, experience, and expertise that fit the team goal *and* who have the ability to live up to the defined mission.

When the German national team under Klinsmann, and later under Jürgen Löw, was being established and developed further, only players who fit the team mission and had the right skills sets and talents were invited. Super-successful players considered too self-centered, arrogant, and not modest enough to live up to the values in the team mission were removed from the team or not invited, despite their individual achievements.

Working With an Existing Team

When a team leader takes over an existing team (which is what usually happens), I recommend that they define the team vision, goals, and mission with the team and that they discuss the ways everyone fits the agreed *reason to exist*. However, if, as team leader, you feel that you have people on board who will not fit this agreed scenario, make all the painful decisions about letting people go as early as possible. One person who is not a team player is enough to undermine a team's performance.

Clarity About Roles and Responsibilities

Gain clarity about who is on the team and who plays which role as soon as possible after taking over an existing team. Richard Hackman, who is Professor of Social and Organizational Psychology at Harvard University, analyzed the data of more than 120 top management teams from around the world. Unsurprisingly, he found that almost every senior team he studied thought it had clarity regarding people on the team and the roles for which they were responsible. Yet, when he asked the members to describe their team, fewer than 10% agreed about who was on it and who exactly played which role. And these were teams of senior executives! (Hackman, as cited in Coutu, 2009)

High-performing teams have clarity about who plays which role in the team and who is responsible for which tasks. These well-functioning teams understand how their individual tasks align with the team goals. The leader encourages these individuals to deploy their strengths and areas of interest when defining individual and collective roles and responsibilities, which further increases motivation in the team. Conversations about these responsibilities are an ongoing part of business life in high-performing teams to ensure that people are aligned with one another.

Paradoxically, setting clear boundaries regarding roles and responsibilities is the prerequisite for creating space for people to be creative and innovative. Within these boundaries, people should find multiple opportunities for autonomous decision-making and self-directed activities.

Clarity about roles and responsibilities is critical for success, since it:

- improves collaboration between members
- allows members to work independently and stay task-focused
- avoids duplication of efforts
- creates awareness of each member's talents
- applies individuals' strengths to key tasks
- clarifies how the team can work toward the same goals.

TEAM SIZE

As a team gets bigger, the number of links that need to be managed between members increases greatly. Managing the links between members makes teamwork difficult. A rule of thumb we recommend is to avoid a double-digit number. Having a huge leadership team that, for instance, includes all the chief executive officer's direct reports might be counterproductive. There are many cases where the collaboration within a large team, particularly in truly creative endeavors, is an obstacle to excellent decision making and high performance (Hackmann, as cited in Coutu 2009).

Success Factor 3: Modern and Collective Leadership

The third success factor of a high-performing team depends on the quality of the team leadership. A team needs a strong and capable leader at the top, a strong sense of collective leadership, and the required competencies in the team members.

Let us start with the first: *What does a strong, capable team leader look like? What qualities should he or she have?* While there are a great many possible answers to these questions, most executives and leadership experts around the world agree that effective leadership is above all adaptive, flexible, and contextual. This means that effective leadership considers factors such as the culture in which you operate (national culture, company culture, and team culture) and the psychological make-up of the people with whom you deal.

All high-performing teams I have studied and coached over the years had leaders at the top and players in the team who exhibited adaptive leadership behavior. These team leaders excelled in two qualities: They were capable of diagnosing the leadership needs of the situations in which they were and they deployed the most effective leadership behavior to positively impact how these situations developed. Thus, they knew when and how to use which leadership style in order to help their teams and their organizations become the best they could be.

There are a number of leadership concepts with which team leaders can work to polish their leadership capabilities. I suggest the concept based on the work of Daniel Goleman, who became famous with his best-selling book on emotional intelligence.

Goleman (2000) differentiates between six leadership styles, which we will now briefly describe in Table 5.1.

Research shows that some of these styles have a positive and energizing effect on the climate and the development of employees (particularly the visionary, the affiliative, the democratic, and the coaching leadership styles), while other styles (pace-setting and directive) impact negatively on these aspects (Goleman, 2000). However, in practice, we have seen that all styles that are overused can have negative effects. For instance, overusage of a democratic leadership style leads to a lack of speed, energy, and decision making. The most successful leaders—those who achieve outstanding business results and high ratings for their leadership behavior—are capable of executing the styles that best suit situations.

Table 5.1. Six Leadership Styles

Directive Leadership Style	Visionary Leadership Style	Affiliative Leadership Style
This *do what I say* approach can be very effective in a turnaround situation, a natural disaster, or when working with challenging employees. If over-used, a commanding leadership blocks the organization's flexibility and diminishes employee motivation.	A visionary leader takes a *come with me* approach: He or she states the overall goals, yet gives people the freedom to choose their own ways to achieve results. This style works especially well when a business is in a difficult situation. It is less effective when the leader is working with an expert team more experienced than the leader.	The affiliative leader has a *people come first* attitude. This style is particularly useful for building team harmony or increasing morale. But its exclusive focus on praise can allow poor performance to go uncorrected. The affiliative leader rarely offers direct feedback or advice, and so leaves employees unclear about their performance.
Democratic Leadership Style	Pace-setting Leadership Style	Coaching Leadership Style
By giving workers a voice in decisions, democratic leaders build organizational flexibility and responsibility, and help generate fresh ideas. Sometimes the price is endless meetings and confused employees who feel underled. There is a positive impact on the organizational climate, but not as high as one might imagine.	A leader who sets high performance standards and exemplifies them positively impacts on highly competent and self-motivated employees. However, others may feel overwhelmed by the continual demand for strong results and high standards; some will resent this leader's tendency to take over.	This style focuses more on personal development than on immediate work-related tasks. It works well when employees are already aware of their weaknesses and want to improve, but not when they are resistant to changing their ways.

The following quick test is a great way to think about your current leadership behaviors. *Which styles do you use most often and why? Which styles do you use less often? Does your leadership create the outcomes that you want to achieve?* This quick test might be a first step to reflect on how you can further develop yourself as a leader to become more effective.

A Quick Test

Use the scale shown in Table 5.2 to indicate how each statement applies to you. Evaluate each statement honestly and without overthinking it.

Interpreting Your Results

This quick test can give you a first indication of how adaptive your leadership currently is. Please contextualize these results in your current

Table 5.2.   A Quick Text

How often do you apply a **directive leadership style** in the course of a day?	Not often	Sometimes	Quite often
I provide clear instructions about what needs to be done and how.	1	2	3
I make decisions when others are still discussing a subject.	1	2	3
I check and follow up whether my decisions and instructions are carried out.	1	2	3
How often do you apply a **visionary leadership style** in the course of a day?	Not often	Sometimes	Quite often
I make an effort to help others to see the bigger picture and make them aware of how their work contributes to the overall vision of the team and the organization.	1	2	3
I start a conversation, presentation, or meeting by first describing the bigger context of what I have to say.	1	2	3
My thinking is future-oriented and possibility-oriented, and I use these ideas to inspire my people to work towards an improved future.	1	2	3
How often do you apply an **affiliative leadership style** in the course of a day?	Not often	Sometimes	Quite often
I actively try to create harmony among other people and in my team.	1	2	3
I empathize with other people's feelings and make them feel important	1	2	3
Throughout my career I build friendly often long lasting relationships with colleagues and other stakeholders	1	2	3
How often do you apply a **democratic leadership style** in the course of a day?	Not often	Sometimes	Quite often
I encourage my team to get involved in discussions about important decisions and facilitate moments of joint or independent decision-making.	1	2	3
I ask my team to work together on setting team goals.	1	2	3
I share responsibilities with my team and reward team efforts.	1	2	3

(Table continues on next page)

Table 5.2.   (Continued)

How often do you apply a **pace-setting leadership style** in the course of a day?	Not often	Sometimes	Quite often
I set standards for excellence and speed and expect others to do the same.	1	2	3
I role-model excellent work ethics and expect others to follow this example.	1	2	3
I notice poor performance by others and follow up immediately.	1	2	3
How often do you apply a **coaching leadership style** in the course of a day?	Not often	Sometimes	Quite often
I ask others open questions that make them think about solving a problem and help them to develop their problem-solving skills.	1	2	3
I ask more often open, intelligent questions than I offer advice or solutions.	1	2	3
I take time to explore the career ambitions, long-term goals, and talents of others so that I can give them the support they need to develop in the most efficient ways.	1	2	3

Note: 1 = Not often; 2 = Sometimes; 3 = Quite often.

work situation to reflect on the question whether you currently have the balance right. For a more comprehensive picture, you would also need solid feedback from the people you lead and others around you (i.e., your peers and your boss).

COLLECTIVE LEADERSHIP

It is crucial to have a strong sense of collective leadership in the team. This means that people hold each other accountable for their actions and their behaviors. An important leader task is to build a sense of collective leadership by sharing responsibility with team members and ensuring that all five success factors of a high-performing team are considered when building the team. A sign of collective leadership is when people voluntarily coach and support each other without involving the team leader.

Success Factor 4: Establishing a *We* Culture

One of the outstanding characteristics of all high-performing teams with which I have worked is that they have established a successful *we* culture. In a *we* culture, all the team members generally work toward a set of common goals, support each other, have fun along the way, and often celebrate successes together. They are comfortable sharing insights and information with one another and with upper management, hold each other accountable, and are highly motivated and results-driven. The team members trust one another and have a constructive approach to conflicts. If they were to describe the team atmosphere, they would emphasize the great team spirit.

Negative Effects of a *Me* Culture in a Team

Building a *we* culture is one of the five success factors of any high-performing team. Building and maintaining this culture is a key leader task. However, it's not as simple as it might sound. In practice, I often see a me-centric team culture and its negative effects on a team's performance.

A research project by Professor Paul Harvey (2010) of the University of New Hampshire on generational differences concluded that me-centric employees:

1. have problems accepting negative feedback
2. are less likely to see the positive aspects their job
3. have exaggerated expectations about themselves and their work
4. are more likely to engage in workplace conflicts
5. are more likely to blame others for whatever happens on the job
6. are more likely to take credit for other people's work
7. are considered less effective at leading teams and bringing people together.

The Three Pillars of a *We* Culture

The three building blocks of a *we* culture can be summarized as follows:

1. Clarity about goals: As noted, every high-performing team needs clear individual and team goals. Without clear individual goals, single team members might be demotivated, without clear team goals there is no cooperative interaction between team members. When assigning tasks and defining job roles, clarify how the work contributes to the team goals everyone contributes to individually.
2. Agreement on mission and team values: I have already emphasized the importance of having a team mission or a set of team values on which everybody agrees and tries to live up to. Two values have to be part of your mission statement if you want to build a we-centric culture: (a) cooperation and (b) accountability. If you do not focus

on teamwork and cooperation between team members, you are unlikely to excel in this area. On the other hand, accountability is the value directly linked to the business results that a team or the entire organizations achieves. Be outspoken about the culture when hiring new team members.

3.   Be conscious of what you reward: If your recognition activities focus on individual results rather than team results, you will most likely nourish individual success at the expense of team success. If you verbally emphasize team cooperation, but reward individual achievements or egoistic behavior, you are undermining your efforts to build a high-performing team. However, as a leader you need to find a balance between building a *we* culture on the one hand and acknowledging the part individuals play. Most people want to be part of a team, but they also want to be recognized for their individual efforts (Glaser, 2005).

Building Trust

The prerequisite for going from *me* to *we* is a foundation of trust between the team members. The trust level in any relationship determines the quality. This holds true for personal and business relationships. Teams who build trust early on experience fewer conflicts later and are more likely to develop their full performance potential. The trust equation (Maister, 2000) is a concept the managers with whom I worked found very useful. This trust equation highlights key factors that determine trust levels in the team or in one-on-one relationships (see Figure 5.2).

Credibility relates to our words, and is revealed in our credentials and honesty. It focuses on a person's technical, job-related expertise and capabilities.

Reliability relates to our actions and is revealed when we keep our promises. *Can I trust this person to deliver on time and in the manner they promised?*

Intimacy relates to our emotions. People feel safe talking about difficult agendas. *Can I trust this person to keep information confidential? Do they reveal something about themselves?*

Self-orientation relates to our caring and is revealed in our focus (us or them?)

COACHING FOR *WE*

Once you have started creating a *we* culture, coaching is an effective tool to involve your employees in the process. Ask your employees to identify best practices, processes, and tactics that can improve the company

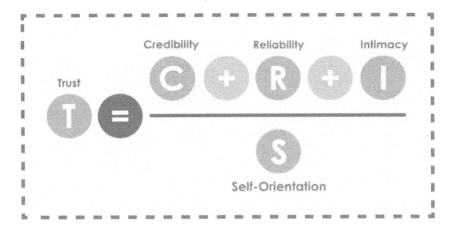

Figure 5.2.   The trust equation.

performance. Sharing ideas and best practices is an essential way to leverage talent, inspire commitment, and nourish the *we* culture in the team. Colleagues who learn from one another are more inclined to create a *we* culture together (Glaser, 2005).

Success Factor 5: Effective External and Internal Communication

The fifth success factor of a high-performing team is the quality of its internal and external communication. We describe this quality as we-centric, effective, efficient, and resource-friendly. People focus on communication that adds value to all involved in the communication. The key question is: *Does the right message go to the right people at the right time using the best means of communication that fits the purpose?* In 90% of cases, the answer is *no*, which is a tragedy in modern business life. Billions of working hours are wasted by people writing billions of emails that collectively only waste people's time. This can be avoided when people think carefully about what value their communication adds to others and themselves. Table 5.3 summarizes the most important characteristics of a we-centric communication culture, in contrast to a me-centric communication culture, which is often ineffective, inefficient, and resource-unfriendly.

Constructive Conflicts About Subject Matter

Another facet of productive, healthy communication is that people feel safe enough to approach conflict about a subject in proactive, constructive

Table 5.3.   We-Centric Communication Culture

We-Centric Communication	*Me-Centric Communication*
Principle of attraction: We build on common ground. We build a future together.	**Principle of assertion:** I state my needs or wants; I make a proposal; I persist; I offer logical arguments why *my way is the highway.*
We-centric attitude: I am aware of you.	**Me-centric attitude:** I am aware of myself and my needs.
Push and pull are in balance: Pushing (talking) and pulling (asking and listening) information in conversations are in balance.	**Push and pull are out of balance:** Focus on sending information; mainly talking, less listening.
Building bridges: I recap what you say; I explore your arguments, views, and feelings and offer my arguments, views, and feelings.	**Logical arguments**: I make proposals, I state logical reasons, and if you are not convinced, I provide more of the same.
Share the *big picture* and the right amount of detailed information. Start by setting down overarching goals.	**Share only detailed information**: *Big picture* information about changes are shared too late in the process.
Encourage people to learn from mistakes. Admitting when you are wrong can turn a mistake into a learning moment.	**Finger-pointing:** Openly blaming people for making mistakes.
Recognition: Verbally recognize others' achievements.	**Criticism:** Only speaking up when criticizing others.
Share power: At meetings, give the lead to your employees, so that they learn how to lead and communicate effectively.	**Hold on to power:** Dominating every conversation and meeting.
Encourage feedback: As everyone (including the boss) receives regular feedback, everyone grows faster.	**Discourage feedback:** Feedback proceeds from the leader to the employees only, not vise versa.
Turn attention of the team inwards and outwards to the organization and the customers.	**Turn attention inward only:** For instance, to the boss.
Role-modeling behavior: Communicate by role-modeling desired behavior.	**Not walking the talk:** Asking others to change doesn't create change. Show, do not tell.
E-mail hygiene: Ensure that the right message gets to the right people at the right time.	**E-mail madness:** Unstructured e-mails, copying everyone in, wasting people's time.

ways. I encourage team leaders to select team members for a diversity of perspectives. Innovation happens in the clash of diverging ideas. If team members are mature enough to handle conflict, the team will be rewarded. In suboptimal teams, conflict is avoided, resulting in a false sense of agreement.

Balanced Communication With Relevant Stakeholders

In business, no one succeeds alone. This also holds true for teams. No team can work in isolation. Teams always need the support of the organization and that of other teams if they are to succeed. Teams need to ensure that they are visible in the organization and that their successes are recognized. To ensure organizational support and to create win-win situations across the organization, teams need to establish effective and efficient external communication methods (as we have suggested here). Teams should put in the effort to identify their most important stakeholders. A team's ultimate task is to work toward satisfying its internal and/or external customers, as defined in its team vision and the team and individual goals. Effective communication with these customers is a cornerstone of a team's overall success.

CONCLUSION

The five success factors of a high-performing team are interdependent. It is fair to say that factors 1 and 2 should be looked after first when building your team. Regardless of the scores you receive in the following team assessment, know that a high-performing team needs constant work, because without it, even the best ones go off track. As a leader, you need to create space for this kind of leadership work if you want a team that produces better and faster results than an average team. Well-organized and professionally facilitated off-site meetings are among the best and proven interventions to bring teams on track in keeping with all five levels of *The Five Success Factors of a High-performing Team* pyramid.

Paradoxically, as a leader, you need to develop the discipline to regularly stop to think and discuss the *how* of working together before you can continue to achieve the results (the *what*) that you are all striving for at high speed. High-performing teams work smarter, not harder.

TEAM ASSESSMENT

This questionnaire is a straightforward diagnostic tool to help you evaluate your team's performance along the five success factors. If possible, have all team members complete it, and review the results, discussing different responses and identifying clear implications for the team. Use the scale shown in Table 5.4 to indicate how each statement applies to you. Evaluate each statement honestly and without overthinking it.

Table 5.4. Team Assessment

Success factor 1: Team vision, team goals, and team mission	Not at all	Sometimes	Agree
In our team, we have a set of clearly defined team goals, and everyone contributes equally towards achieving them.	1	2	3
Our team vision sets standards for excellence and inspires team members to perform at the best of their abilities.	1	2	3
We have clearly defined behavioral standards and values that we all live up to in daily business life.	1	2	3
Success factor 2: People and roles	Not at all	Sometimes	Agree
Roles and responsibilities are clearly defined based on the individuals' strengths.	1	2	3
Everyone knows how the individual and team responsibilities contribute towards the team's overall success.	1	2	3
Within the team's clearly defined boundaries, members have enough space to be creative and make autonomous decisions in their areas of responsibility.	1	2	3
Success factor 3: Modern and collective leadership	Not at all	Sometimes	Agree
The team leader knows when to use which leadership style to apply to achieve maximum results and to create a good working atmosphere.	1	2	3
Team members coach and support one another to stay on track with the team's goals and mission.	1	2	3
There is a strong sense of collective leadership, with people holding each other accountable for their actions.	1	2	3
Success factor 4: Establishing a we culture	Not at all	Sometimes	Agree
In our team, we have a great level of trust.	1	2	3
Team members feel safe enough to engage in healthy conflict about subject matter.	1	2	3
The team has a great team spirit and everyone supports one another.	1	2	3

(Table continues on next page)

Table 5.4.   (Continued)

Success factor 5: Effective external and internal communication	Not at all	Sometimes	Agree
Our communication is balanced. We effectively communicate inwardly and outwardly (to internal and external customers).	1	2	3
The team leader and team members learn from their mistakes and proactively seek feedback from one another.	1	2	3
Communication in the team is efficient. Everyone repeatedly reflects on the question: Do I send the right message to the right people at the right time using the best means of communication that fits the purpose?	1	2	3

Notes: 1 = I do not agree at all; 2 = I sometimes agree; 3 = I agree.

INTERPRETING YOUR RESULTS

It is less about the exact scores you and your team achieve with this questionnaire than about using this tool to stimulate in-depth conversations with your team members in order to create a shared understanding about where you are at on your journey toward a high-performing team and what work still needs to be done for you to attain the desired state. This tool is best used as a regular *health check* (at least once or twice a year).

REFERENCES

Boundless. (2016). *The role of teams in Organizations*. Boundless Management.

Coutu, D. (2009). *Why teams don't work*. Harvard Business Review issue of May.

Glaser, J. (2005). *Creating WE: Change I-thinking to we-thinking & build a healthy thriving organization*. Avon, MA: Platinum Press.

Goleman, D. (2000, March–April). Leadership that gets results. *Harvard Business Review*.

Harvey, P. (2010). Entitlement and Generation Y. https://vimeo.com/11748765

Keller, G., & Papsan, J. (2013). *The ONE thing: The surprisingly simple truth behind extraordinary results*.

Maister, D. (2001). *The trusted advisor*. Free Press.

CHAPTER 6

NEGOTIATION SKILLS FOR LEADERS

Transaction Utility in Negotiation

Matthew Mulford

OBJECTIVE

Excellent leaders must be effective negotiators. They must understand that how people feel about a deal can be as important as the underlying financials. In this chapter, we see how the distinction between *transaction* utility and *acquisition* utility can help leaders make sense of negotiation behavior that would not be expected in standard negotiation approaches. Once leaders understand the interaction of these two factors, they can more skilfully provide productive *reference points* during negotiations.

UNDERSTANDING CONSUMPTION CHOICES

Imagine yourself in the following situation. You have been trying to decide where to go on holiday for weeks. You have finally narrowed down the options to two—a week in either Dubai or the Maldives. You know you

Advanced Leadership Insights: How to Lead People and Organizations to Ultimate Success
pp. 73–83
Copyright © 2017 by Information Age Publishing
73

will enjoy both, but would prefer to go to the Maldives. However, it is much more expensive than going to Dubai. You are at home and you have the two package holidays side by side on your computer screen. All you need to do is click on the "purchase" button of either and you are ready to go … how do you make the choice? What is the internal calculus ins your mind to help you decide?

Understanding how people make these types of choices is very important to any business. Unsurprisingly, academics have long been thinking, studying, and theorizing about this type of problem. Understanding consumption choices is key to marketing, advertising, sales, pricing, and much more.

Since at least the start of the 20th century, traditional economics has focused on the concepts of opportunity costs and acquisition utility to model consumption choice. Utility describes how good (positive utility) or bad (negative utility) something makes us feel. *Acquisition utility* is the amount of utility derived from consuming or using an acquired object. *Opportunity costs* is the amount of positive utility we forego by *not* doing the next best thing. In our holiday choice example, a visit to Dubai or the Maldives will each produce a certain amount of positive utility.[1] If you were to go to Dubai, you give up the extra utility you would get from going to the Maldives, but would save money. Is the saving worth the lost utility? Economists have traditionally answered "it depends"—it depends on how much extra utility you would derive by spending the money on something else. That extra utility is then added onto the total utility calculation of the Dubai choice. Standard economics would say you need to look at all possible options for spending your saved money in order to accurately calculate which choice has the higher *consumer surplus*; the acquisition utility minus the opportunity cost.

At first glance, this seems to make some sense. When making the Dubai versus Maldives choice, most of us would look at the difference in cost and think about how much the savings would be worth. Now, you might not consider all possible alternatives—who has the time for that!—but you might look at the most salient ones. Let us say, for instance, that going to the Maldives would mean you could not pay your children's school fees. The negative utility of harming your children's educational opportunities may make the decision for Dubai an easy one. On the other hand, if the difference would mean that you would have to keep your current car for another year before you purchased a new one, you might decide that a week in a tropical paradise, compared to a week in Dubai, might be worth the delay. Notice I said "at first glance." A key problem with this approach is that it ignores the fact that how the purchase makes us *feel* can profoundly influence our consumption choices.

It Was Such a Great Deal, I Had to Buy It

My mother loves to cook; naturally, I love her food. Recently, at her house, I and noticed a 2.25kg container of paprika in her cupboard. Paprika tends to be purchased and used in small quantities. A jar would typically contain 25g to 40g. Two and a quarter kilograms of paprika is a *lot* of paprika. Typical recipes call for 3g to 5g. I asked my mother why she had so much paprika. She explained that the last time she was at her local store she bought a 35g bottle of paprika for $3.85.[2] She had bought the 2.25kg container of the same brand for $15.00 during a recent visit to a regional hypermarket. It was such a great deal, "she could not resist." But here's the point. On average, my mother uses at most about one 35g bottle of paprika a year. She is 74. She now has enough paprika to last until she is 138!

Unfortunately, even if I assume my mother will live to be the oldest woman in the world, the maximum recommended shelf-life for dried herbs is about 3 to 4 years, limiting the value of her mountain of paprika. The maximum acquisition utility of the massive bottle of paprika at my mother's current rate of use is equal to about 3.5 years. In the 2.25kg size, this cost $15.00. In the 35g size, the cost is about $13.50. By acquisition utility terms only, my mother has made a mistake.[3] She would save $1.50 by buying a 35g bottle every year for 3 years. Yet, she was *delighted* by her purchase—something I was not about to dispute—because the purchase had made her *feel* good.

This feeling is what Richard Thaler (1983) calls *transaction utility*. The act of buying such cheap paprika (an equivalent price of $0.23 for 35g versus $3.85) was a source of good feelings, apart from any use she would ever get from such a massive quantity. There can also be negative transactional utility, and it can have just as a profound effect on consumer behavior and therefore on pricing strategy as the *good deal effect*.

Sonic Automotive is one of the largest used car dealers in the United States. In 2014, it announced a new sales policy—no haggling over the price of its cars. Jeff Dyke, Sonic's executive vice president of operations, explained the move as follows: "Negotiations going back and forth and all that crap—we want to get out of all that. We don't see a need for it, and neither does the consumer" (Wilson, 2014). But why would a consumer want to forego a chance at a lower price through negotiation? In acquisition utility terms, this makes little sense. I should get the best price I can and can then compare the utility I could derive from other purchases of the same amount. Yet, here is a retailer publicly advertising a strict change in sales strategy—it will no longer consider lowering its prices as a result of discussion with a potential buyer.

In transactional utility, this makes perfect sense. For many people, fixed prices mean that they avoid any chances of negative transactional utility if/when they find out that someone else got a better deal. For many, the prospect of a slightly higher fixed price is worth the elimination of the potential negative utility felt if they were to discover that their deal was not as good as what others have received.

Note that transactional utility *only* comes into play if there is some contrast between the price paid and the price offered somewhere else. For my mother, the massive amount of paprika was a deal because she knew the price for the 35g jar. For car buyers, it's the price others pay for the same cars. Without any kind of comparator, there is no way to know what is a good or a bad deal, and acquisition utility is what matters. Retailers provide comparators all the time in an effort to create transactional utility for their customers. There is often a recommended retail price followed by some "discount" price. Creating these "savings" is a way to create transactional utility. For instance, if the Maldives holiday was offered at a "last minute" special rate of 50% of the normal price, then all other things being equal—including the price difference with the Dubai trip being exactly the same—many more people would choose the Maldives. What value we compare our purchase to becomes a key to predicting transactional utility. Different values can lead to very dramatic changes in the way a deal is perceived. A sequence of events I observed between a group of executives on an executive MBA course in Shanghai will illustrate this case.

Jonathon, Jason, and a number of other students were sitting in a hotel lobby discussing what they had done on one of their few free afternoons in the city. Jonathon was describing a "deal" that he had received from a local tailor—three beautifully made custom-tailored dress shirts for the equivalent of $100. He figured that the shirts would have cost him at least three times that amount in London, his home town. Jonathon was experiencing high acquisition and transaction utility from his purchase and was feeling good sharing his good fortune with his colleagues. Jason then congratulated him on a "pretty good deal." Jonathon asked what Jason meant by "pretty good." Jason described how he had been given a three-shirt deal, from the same tailor, for $65. Jonathon's anger was both intense and surprising. His face turned deep red and he demanded to know how Jason had managed it. Jason described how he had first been quoted the same price as Jonathon; it was only after he had left the shop and come back with competitive prices from other tailors in the same street that he had been offered the better deal. In the end, Jonathon took his shirts back to the tailor and was furious when he was denied Jason's deal.

Jonathon's reference point had changed from the price paid in London to the price paid by Jason. The shirts had not changed; the price paid for the shirts had not changed; the quality of the shirts had not changed; Jonathon's positive utility stream from using the shirts had not changed. What had changed was his perception of the quality of the deal. And that was most important.

APPLICATION: NEGOTIATION

In *Getting to Yes*, perhaps the most-read book on negotiation ever, Roger Fisher and Willam Ury (2011) applied an acquisition utility framework to negotiation. Almost anyone who has ever had any formal negotiation training is familiar with the term BATNA or "best alternative to a negotiated agreement." As part of the preparation phase of any negotiation, Fisher and Ury urge people to carefully define the value of their BATNA in order to be able to value a potential negotiated outcome. If the deal is worth less than your alternative, you should walk away; if it is better than your alternatives, you should accept the deal.

Identifying a BATNA is the same as identifying opportunity costs. In each, you compare one course of action with the value of what would happen if you chose something else. When choosing between Dubai and the Maldives, we compared one choice: the Maldives with the best alternative, Dubai. We need to value the different alternatives in some metric to allow comparison. In the holiday choice, it is utility. In negotiations, we generally convert our BATNA into some monetary value and compare it to the monetary value of the deal on the table. We know from decades of negotiation research that carefully defining a BATNA is vital to help avoid deals that leave you worse off, or turning down deals that leave you better off than your alternatives. BATNA analysis and traditional economic consumer choice theories are essentially the same—and they both tend to ignore the role of transactional utility.

Negotiations can be divided into two types; single-issue *distributive* negotiations and multi-issue *integrative* negotiations. Let us first look at transaction utility in the distributive case.

Distributive Negotiations

Distributive negotiations generally refer to those that divide up the amount of surplus created from a single-issue negotiation. The surplus is created by the difference in the value of each negotiator's BATNA. Let us say, for instance, that I want to sell you my house. I may decide that I must receive a minimum of price $X (a *reserve* price) for my house based on my BATNA. You may decide that you are willing to pay up to a maximum of $Y for my house based on yours. The overlap between $Y and $X, often defined as the *zone or possible agreement* (ZOPA), defines the total value which will be any deal agreed between $X and $Y. Our negotiation will determine how that surplus is distributed. If we both freely agree to the deal, it must mean that the buyer receives some value greater than $X and the seller some value greater than $Y. Given that $X and $Y are meant to be based on the respective best alternatives for the buyer and the seller, both should be happy with the deal. But this is not always the case. Some "win-win" negotiations make people mad, sad, or resentful. And, as we saw above, the transactional utility derived from a deal depends on what is used as the reference point and can profoundly affect our behavior. An example follows:

Imagine that Owen decides to buy his teenage son a car. After carefully shopping around, he finds a used car at a dealer with a reasonable sticker price—$12,000. Owen goes to the dealer and after a long negotiation, the latter agrees to sell the car for $10,000. Based on his analysis of the market for similar cars, Owen would have been willing to pay $11,500 and, so, is quite happy (high transaction utility) with the deal. Now, imagine this purchase took place in a country where Owen is an expat and his immigration status is tied to his employment. If he loses his job, he also loses his legal right to remain in the country. One week after he purchases his son's car, Owen is told that, owing to serious budget cuts, he is being made redundant, effective immediately. Three days later he receives a letter from the immigration services informing him that has 1 month from the date of his termination to leave the country.

Because it is too expensive to transport back to his home country, Owen must now try to sell the car he had bought only 10 days ago. He takes the car back to the dealer and explains the situation; the dealer offers to buy back the car for $6,500. Owen is shocked at the offer. Thinking that the car must be worth at least $10,000 to the dealer, Owen is not prepared to have him gain $3,500 in such a short time for doing nothing. Notice that according to traditional BATNA analysis, how much the other receives should not affect Owen's decision to accept or reject the dealer's offer. It "should" only be based on what Owen believes is his BATNA— what happens if he does not sell the car to the dealer *on that day*. Let us assume that he thinks he can easily sell the car for more than $6,500. After all, he knows that $10,000 was a good deal just 10 days ago. His decision to reject the dealer's offer may yet fit the BATNA approach.[4]

Owen places an advert in the local newspaper; after a week, a potential private buyer comes to look at the car. He asks Owen why he wishes to sell. Owen tells him the story, including the purchase price, and offers to sell the car for $8,500. The potential buyer makes a counteroffer of $7,000. Owen is again angry at the offer and, knowing that the car is worth at least $10,000, he rejects it. Why is Owen angry? Because he continues to use the reference point of his $10,000 purchase price as the car's "value." Selling it for $7,000 would produce large amounts of negative transaction utility, even if it is better than his now known alternative of $6,500. But Owen is hopeful. Surely, someone will buy his car closer to its "real" value.

Another 2 weeks go by and Owen's ad attracts no other buyers. He swallows his pride and calls the private buyer, who now offers to pay him $5,000. Clearly, this man is taking advantage of Owen's situation; Owen says no. Owen calls back dealer, who now offers only $4,500. Again, Owen rejects the offer—it is just too unfair. In a few days, Owen and his family must leave the country. He is now desperate and is willing to take a loss with the dealer. He returns the next day; the dealer offers Owen only $3,000. At his point, Owen is so angry, he decides to not sell the car at all. He leaves it in the street outside his now vacant apartment and the keys and ownership papers inside as a gift to whoever moves in next.

Throughout the time Owen attempted to sell his car, his alternatives were degrading; his potential buyers knew this. So why does he not ever sell? Because he is trapped by his reference point of $10,000. Agreeing on a much lower deal would leave him feeling cheated. In the end, we know that this negative transactional utility must be worse than a loss of $3,000—the amount he turned down in order to give away the car.

Potential deals that are perceived to be unfair or unreasonable are often rejected even when they will create acquisition utility—that is, they would take place within ZOPA. In the case of Owen's car, this led to a sub-optimal outcome for *both* Owen and his potential buyers. The buyer might not have been able to bring himself to buy a car for more than $7,000 because he knew it would be worth less as time went on. The act of paying more than $7,000 for an asset now when he thinks he can acquire it later for substantially less makes any higher price feel like a loss. This might have been avoided if the parties had successfully shifted the subjectively defined reference points. For instance, the dealer might have been explicit about how much he would pay for the car on the last day and the decrease from his initial offer for every day that passed. If Owen thought, "I can get $7,000 today or $4,000 two weeks from now," the $3,000 gain from selling now might have eliminated the pain of the $3,000 loss from the initial $10,000. The point here is that the parties' experienced transactional utility must be considered in the formulation of the negotiation strategies. The narratives one uses to frame one's offers should reflect the need for the other party to feel good about the deal, or value-creating agreements are at risk. The subjectively defined and therefore malleable reference point generates amounts of transactional utility that will have the effect of altering the de facto ZOPA.

Integrative Negotiation

Integrative negotiations deal with multiple issues over which the nego-tiators have different intensities of preferences. Unlike in distributive negotiations where the amount of surplus to be created in the negotiation is fixed, in integrative negotiations the surplus is a function of the struc-ture of the deal. A simple example follows.

Company A wants to sell Company B 1,000 units of Product A. The price per unit sold and the delivery date are both negotiable. Let us say that B negotiates an agreement to pay A $100 per unit for delivery of all units within 1 month. Assume that B would have been willing to pay $110 per unit for delivery of all units. This was based on an estimate of costs from alternative suppliers. B is indifferent to delivery time as long as it receives all units within two months. Thus, the deal creates $10,000 worth of acquisition utility for B. Assume that A would have been willing to settle for a price of $90 per unit for delivery within 1 month (based on alterna-tive buyers and costs). However, to make the 1-month deadline, A will have to pay an additional $5,000 in overtime costs. Thus, the negotiated deal also creates $5,000 worth of acquisition utility for A. Let us call this Deal 1.

There is clearly scope for a better deal for *both* players. Assume that A explains about the extra production costs of $5,000 and offers B a price of $97.50 per unit with the order due for completion within 2 months—Deal 2. A incurs no additional production costs and its total monetary surplus jumps from $5,000 to $7,500 ($97.50 – $90.00 × 1,000 units). B, as the buyer, is also better off. B now receives a monetary surplus of $12,500, up from the $10,000 from Deal 1. If the parties can move from Deal 1 to Deal 2, both parties will gain $2,500—an example of trading across issues to create integrative negotiation potential. In the classic literature on negotiation, this is called an efficiency or *Pareto* improvement—at least one party is better off and none is made worse off by the move from Deal 1 to Deal 2.[5] How might transactional utility make such deals harder?

Let us assume that Deal 2 was struck. It is now 3 months later, and B again begins negotiations with A on a potential new order. However, the situation has changed. Imagine that B uses A's units as component parts for something it produces. B has a contract with a buyer who offers a bonus for delivery within one month. Therefore, if A can deliver all its units to B within one month, they have a value $130 each to B. If the deadline is missed, the value drops back to $110. During the course of the negotiations, A discovers the change in B's situation and offers Deal 3: $115 per unit for 1,000 units for delivery within 1 month. Deal 3 offers B an acquisition utility of $15,000 ($130 – $115 × 1,000)—higher than Deal 2. It offers A an acquisition utility of $20,000 ($115 – $90 × 1,000 units – the $5,000 cost of overtime)—again higher than Deal 2. Deal 3 is a Pareto improvement on Deal 2; yet, B turns it down. Why?

B knows that A had initially offered to provide product X for $100 per unit within 1 month. The $115 is much, much higher for no apparent reason! Or, it might use Deal 2's $97.50 unit cost as its reference point. B knows that A's additional costs to make the delivery within 1 month is $5,000. B figures—correctly—the per unit cost increase of the expedited delivery to be $5 per unit ($5,000 divided across the 1,000 units, in which case it might expect a per unit cost of $102.50 ($97.50 + $5). But A is seeking to charge B $115 per unit. B reasons that A is claiming a large part of the surplus generated by delivery to its buyer within 1 month—a surplus A had no part in creating. B finds the price increase unjustifiable and unacceptable and says no to A's offer.

Instead, B reaches Deal 4 with a competitor of A for an order 1,000 units at $96.00 per unit to be delivered over 2 months, creating $14,000 (an acquisition utility of $110 – $96 × 1,000 units). B reasons that the negotiation with A had been a success of sorts. It had led it to negotiate with a new supplier, and the new deal is cheaper than A's at 2 months—a saving of $1,500. B is forced to forego the bonus for early delivery of its product with its new client, but is delighted to call A to tell B they will no longer need to transact with it. Clearly, the negative transactional utility that would have been experienced by B if it had gone with Deal 3 must be worse than foregoing $1,000 ($14,000 from Deal 4 versus $15,000 from Deal 3).

Integrative negotiations often involve pushing one issue to an extreme position in exchange for an extreme value on another. In classic negotiation analyses, these tradeoffs across issues create value and increase the efficiency of deals, implying that no one should resist a shift. However, this ignores potential negative transaction utility that can result from deals that include extreme values that seem unfair or unjustified. As with distributive negotiations, one should take care during the negotiations to set reference points in such a way as to increase subjective transaction utility. In the case of B, the focus on the overall value created for it by Deal 3 versus Deal 2, rather than how much more A benefited from such a move, might have allowed it to avoid the negative transaction utility and thereby might have increased the overall utility for both parties.

FINAL THOUGHTS

Standard negotiation analysis, with its emphasis on BATNAs, negotiation surplus, and Pareto efficiency tends to ignore how the transaction utility of whatever deal is on offer. How the deal makes people feel is ignored at the negotiators' peril.[6] To go from a good negotiator to an expert negotiator, leaders must integrate concerns for others' transaction utility into their approach and must seek to set reference points that will make people feel good about the deal. Attending to and guarding how the other feels about the deal and the negotiating process can be just as important as designing optimally efficient deals.

NOTES

1. In fact, the choice involves anticipated positive utility. This requires us to make an estimate of the likelihood of the visit producing a certain amount of utility. Because it is uncertain, we must discount each utility calculation by a function of the uncertainty we had about the different possible outcomes. But, for now, let us just keep things simple and assume we know exactly how each holiday will make us feel.
2. All "$" signs in this chapter refer to U.S. dollars.
3. The mistake would be further compounded if we consider the time-discounted cost of money, but that is another story!
4. Note that Owen's use of the $10,000 purchase further compounds the problem, because all subsequent figures are seen as losses. We know that people take more risks to avoid a loss than they would to attempt a gain. Owen is willing to take the risk of attempting to sell the car to avoid a perceived $3,000 loss. For the definitive discussion of how reference points can affect risk attitudes, see Kahneman and Tversky (1979).
5. For the classic discussion of efficiency concepts as applied to distributive versus integrative negotiations, see Raiffa (2002).
6. For a great treatment of this type of approach, see Voss (2016). Voss, a former chief hostage negotiator to the FBI, reveals how paying attention to what I call transitional utility can be a key determinant of the quality of negotiated outcomes in both normal and extreme settings.

REFERENCES

Fisher, R., & Ury, W. (2012). *Getting to yes: Negotiating agreement without giving in* (B. Patton, Ed.). London, England: Random House Business Books.

Kahneman, D., & Tversky, A. (1979). Prospect theory: An analysis of decision under risk. *Econometrica, 47*(2), 263–291.

Raiffa, H. (2002). *Negotiation analysis: The art and science of collaborative decision making*. Cambridge, MA: Harvard University Press.

Thaler, R. (1983). Transaction utility theory. In R. P. Bagozzi & A. M. Tybout (Eds.), *Advances in consumer research* (Vol. 10, pp. 229–232). Ann Arbor, MI: Association for Consumer Research.

Voss, C. (2016). *Never split the difference: Negotiating as if your life depended on it*. New York, NY: HarperCollins.

Wilson, A. (2014, May 14). Sonic plans to leave haggling far behind. *Automotive News*. Retrieved from http://www.autonews.com/article/20140503/RETAIL07/305059984/sonic-plans-to-leave-haggling-far-behind

CHAPTER 7

REFLECTIVE LEADERSHIP

Successfully Leading Your Team in a Complex World

Felix Müller and Ragna Kirberg

OBJECTIVE

We first explain why people react with reduced confidence in managing challenges caused by the increased complexity and uncertainty of today's world. We then invite you to discover how, as a leader, you can support your people in re-building confidence by using *reflective leadership*, specifically *reflection by thinking and feeling*, and ultimately reaching your and their goals.

INTRODUCTION

The world we live and conduct business in is often described as volatile, uncertain, complex, and ambiguous (VUCA).

People in the West are seeing that job security and guaranteed wealth are beginning to fade, and the system of right and wrong being replaced by *a dynamic and ever-changing system.*

Advanced Leadership Insights: How to Lead People and Organizations to Ultimate Success
pp. 85–100
Copyright © 2017 by Information Age Publishing

Life in the 20th century was mostly predictable and consisted of applying ("best") practices to new situations, leading to emotional stability. Today, the fast-changing environment makes business transformation processes necessary, and strategic goals have to be challenging so as to guarantee a company's survival. This sometimes leads to unexpected and non-sustainable results, which harm the company in the long run. The Volkswagen scandal about manipulated emission results is one example of this.

All of this can lead to negative emotional arousal and anxiety, which translates into stress and the fight-or-flight reaction humans acquired in the Stone Age when seeing a saber-tooth tiger. And, while then people could relax somewhat once such as threat no longer prevailed, people today have difficulties stepping out of stress mode. This stress may paralyze an entire organization when decisions are no longer made or are delegated upwards. People then neither fight nor flee; they just sit there as if waiting to be eaten.

Two signs of this increasing stress are the growing rates of burnout and depression: a recent German study showed that between 2004 and 2011, the number of sickness days due to burnout grew by 800%, creating substantial economic damage.

This stress and potential paralysis are caused by a decreasing confidence in being capable of tackling the challenges of today. This presents a major challenge for leadership and the survival and development of organizations. Leaders can contribute to resolving this situation by supporting the people they lead. Reflective leadership is one highly effective answer. It helps finding solutions beyond thinking because it is based on reflection that combines both thinking and feeling. This leads to an increase in confidence, which allows for the achieving of individual and organizational goals. Using our full potential brings out unexpected, creative, and sustainable solutions, which supports people and organizations to do business in healthy ways in these challenging times.

THE THEORY BEHIND IT

Exploring The Drop In Confidence

A popular dictionary defines *confidence* as "a feeling or belief that you can do something well or succeed at something" (Merriam-Webster, 2016). The word is closely linked to *self-efficacy*, defined as "people's beliefs about their capabilities to produce designated levels of performance that exercise influence over events that affect their lives" (Bandura, 1994). In a simple example in football, a person might be asked to share her confidence that she can (capability) score a goal (designated level) when hitting the ball toward the goal from 20 meters away (performance).

Usually, people perform tasks where their confidence is high, that is, they are moderately to highly certain they can do them. These tasks are often referred to as *routine* tasks (note: this also applies to highly demanding professions, such as surgeons for whom open-heart surgery is often routine). The routine tasks are complemented by new tasks that are beyond the ordinary patterns. These tasks are called *challenges*. People facing challenges are less certain that they can do them (as opposed to routine tasks).

When confronted by a challenge, one's body reacts with stress. The challenges puts the body into the fight-or-flight state useful thousand of years ago when a hunter suddenly faced a saber-tooth tiger: to avoid being eaten, the hunter could either fight it or run away. Evolution helped the body to establish patterns that support both options: the focus is on making the hunter strong (to fight) or quick (flee), which means that blood and oxygen are taken out of the brain and put into the muscle areas, which means that the body is partially shutting down the brain.

The likelihood in the 21st century of someone encountering a saber-tooth tiger or similarly dangerous predator in the wild is very low. And the fight nor flight reaction is not useful in the business environment. Yet our body still responds in this way. These reactions can't be overrun: they have served us very well, securing our survival for thousands of years, and are managed through our limbic nervous system. While people sometimes try to do away with these reactions, they always return, Thus, accepting the fact that challenges create stress is a first step in dealing with it.

Confidence as an Indicator of Self-Efficacy

Scientifically, confidence is a measure of self-efficacy: by asking people how confident they are in mastering a challenge on a scale between 0 (*I cannot do at all*) and 10 (*I am very certain I can do it*), they provide an indication of how self-efficacious they are (Bandura, 2006).

Several factors describe the nature and extent of self-efficacy:

- *Subjectivity—self-efficacy is highly subjective and personal.* In the football example, person A's confidence may be at 9, while person B's could be at 2.

- *Case-dependency—self-efficacy levels may vary depending on the area one looks at.* While person A has a high confidence in his football skills, he may assess his confidence in frying an egg to restaurant standards as 0. Each person has an infinite collection of self-efficacies that make up their self-esteem; and even a person with low general self-esteem may have pockets of excellence in which their self-efficacy is high.

- *Perceived capability-focused—not willingness-focused.* The above-mentioned measures inquire into an individual's *capability* of mastering a challenge (*I can do this*) and not their *willingness* (*I will do this*). Thus, confidence clearly refers to someone's *perception* of being able to do something, and not to their *willingness* to do it nor to their *objective capability.*

- *Dynamic—self-efficacy can change.* Confidence is always assessed in the moment based on the full information available to one. As the information changes, so does self-efficacy.

USING *REFLECTION WITH THINKING AND FEELING* TO BUILD SELF-EFFICACY AND CONFIDENCE

As noted, self-efficacy is a subjective phenomenon. Thus, it can only be developed by the person and not by another person on their behalf. However, a leader can support the people he or she leads by accompanying them through a process of building self-efficacy and confidence. We summarize the foundation of this process as *reflection by thinking and feeling*, which brings out an individual's full potential by leveraging their full resources through reflection that uses both intellectual and emotional aspects.

The process is illustrated in Figure 7.1: through a challenge, self-efficacy, which is normally at the *personal routine level* (A) drops to (B) and can then be rebuilt to reach (C), where the person again starts working with confidence using *reflection by thinking and feeling*.

When at (B), if nothing is changed, this level is often described by paralysis, that is, people just sit and wait—in the case of the saber-tooth tiger, this would have meant certain death; in today's businesses, it means losing time and energy and being unable to reach set goals.

The previous discussions showed that all three aspects—confidence, self-efficacy, and challenge—are subjective constructs. Thus, a leader may often only become fully aware of a challenge and the lower confidence once a person already has reached position (B) in Figure 7.1. Since this move cannot be prevented, the leader's job starts at point (B) and is about supporting the other person in starting and doing the journey from (B) to (C).

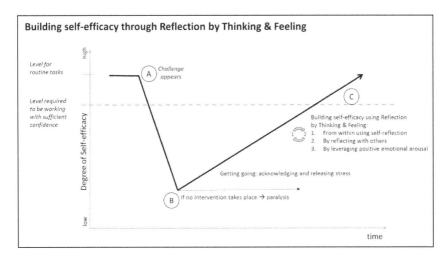

Figure 7.1.   Confidence lost through a stressful challenge is rebuilt using reflection with thinking and feeling.

Getting Going: Acknowledging and Releasing Stress

This journey starts with overcoming the paralysis or fight-or-flight state one is in when experiencing negative emotional arousal in (B). Research shows that this can be done simply by acknowledging and releasing the stress (Lazarus & Folkman, 1984). Another person may simply ask *How do you feel?* and stress is often immediately released. Importantly, the objective is to build for the future and not look back. Here, this means tit suffices to release the stress; no further analysis of what and why it happened is required. This would put the person unnecessarily on the spot and would deviate from the objective to build self-efficacy. Thus, the stressed person receives time and space to let off steam and then moves to the next stage.

Getting People Back Into Confidence

The sociopsychologist Alberto Bandura (1977) was the first to develop a model of self-efficacy and has become the most eminent researcher in the field of self-efficacy (Pajares, 1996). We have further developed his model based on our research, following the key belief that all a person needs to solve a problem or manage a challenge already lies within them—it only has to be found. Our research shows that giving oneself time and space, and spending 15 minutes with thinking and feeling about a challenge yields major changes in confidence without any further intervention by anybody else (Müller, 2016).

This means that, as a leader, you have a powerful and simple tool at hand for both yourself and those you lead: allocate dedicated time and space to reflect on what you and they have within them to manage a challenge.

BUILDING SELF-EFFICACY FROM WITHIN USING SELF-REFLECTION

In challenging situations, people often look to the outside world for support: more information, different viewpoints, and so forth, are sought. However, this disregards the vast repository one has in dealing with life and its challenges. Reflective leadership values our experiences we had and our experiences when observing others dealing with such challenges. Thus, it may be that a person has no experience in a certain area but has observed other people performing a similar task and can access this experience without asking them. A typical example is that a person may not know how to operate the SPSS statistical software package but, by observing others using it, he is confident of being able to do it.

The biggest challenge in using each person's vast resources is in accessing them. Our brain has two ways to manage and store information: the conscious mind and the unconscious mind. The conscious mind is doing what Nobel Prize laureate Daniel Kahneman (2011) refers to as *slow thinking*: It processes information at a speed of 40 Mbps—it is slow, deliberate, and logical-intellectual. The unconscious mind processes information at 11 million Mbps—it is fast, intuitive, and emotional. While Kahneman uses these criteria to describe the processes in *using* the resources, this distinction also applies to the *storage* of information. One can easily understand this difference when one remembers the last time one drove a car: the conscious mind remembers the actions (e.g., going onto the highway or honking. The unconscious mind stores everything around this (i.e., all the surrounding activity, the sounds, smells, and eventually tastes and touches). Thus, all this information is stored and "only" has to be accessed. When dealing with challenges, people often start with analysis: they gather all the available information and then think about it. A typical example of this approach is the question *What do you think about this?* in meetings, pointing to an intellectual answer. This approach is in the tradition of scientific management of the 1910s that looked at people as cogs in an industrial process and also strongly contributed to reflection in the business context being equated with thinking (Dewey, 1910).

Harvard study showed that 15 minutes of reflection a day support an increase in outcome by 20% (Stefano, 2014). Interestingly enough, this was only done using *thinking* and not tapping into the potential of *feeling*.

However, thinking only allows us to access what the working brain can do and only accesses the unconscious mind to a very limited extent. One sees the unconscious mind at work in sudden and most unexpected moments of enlightenment, such as in the shower when one finds a solution to an issue that has been deliberated for weeks: the unconscious mind made the connections (the *sense*) without any further ado by the individual.

While these moments of enlightenment are uncontrolled, we discovered that their logic can be used in a controlled way by simply asking *How do you feel about this? in a meeting*. This approach is also found in the tradition of reflection in the nursing context (Johns, 2009), the approach of emotional intelligence (Goleman, 1996), and the traditions of Buddhist philosophy found in mindfulness (Kabat-Zinn, 2013).

While the individual value of both *thinking* and *feeling* have been recognized for decades by psychologists and sociologists, they have recently been further supported by advances in neurosciences, namely the research by Antonio Damasio (1994, 2000).

Our most recent research shows that combining thinking and feeling leverages the already significant benefits from "just" thinking or feeling in isolation and brings confidence to new statistically significant levels. (Mueller, 2016)

BUILDING SELF-EFFICACY BY REFLECTING WITH OTHERS

Many people may ask: Is this not this what we are doing already in our meetings? However, in the context of reflective leadership, reflection with others is expanded and delivers substantially broader results:

While the traditional reflection process starts with *What do you think about...?*, reflective leadership always also asks *How do you feel about...?* and includes the full spectrum of experiences. Because joint reflection is step 2 in the process, people don't answer these two questions on the spot but prepare: they spent time before joint reflection reflecting individually on the questions. This leads to everyone being prepared, since everyone did the preparation work. This leads to a level starting point for the reflection process and the sharing of experiences.

This process is further strengthened by using pairs as the default mode of reflection: contrary to normal meetings where participants jockey for air-time, political games are played, and quieter or more intuitive participants go unnoticed, reflective leadership uses the one-on-one situation known from coaching to build trustworthy relationships of trust: the two people in a pair commit to sharing their thoughts and feelings about a topic in an appreciative manner. They ask clarifying questions, draw conclusions, and build a relationship as part of a human-human interaction. Each person is in full control of their contribution and only share the parts of their reflection they want. Allowing each other time to speak uninterruptedly and listen attentively creates an atmosphere that is conducive to learning and the building of confidence. At the end, the pairs decide what they want to report to the group.

From a traditional perspective, this may seem time-consuming. Experience shows that a sequence of introduction to a topic, self-reflection, reflection in pairs, and reporting back and discussion in a larger group can easily be accomplished in 30 minutes.

While meetings are the most visible use of this approach, it can be used in any situation where sharing experiences is considered a valuable activity—one can imagine using this approach over lunch.

BUILDING SELF-EFFICACY BY LEVERAGING POSITIVE EMOTIONAL AROUSAL

In his research about self-efficacy, Bandura (1977, 1994, 2006) sees emotional arousal primarily as a negative that lowers self-efficacy through stress when being moved from (A) to (B). However, arousal can be positive or negative. This, people can use positive experiences to increase self-efficacy (Boud, Keogh, & Walker, 1985) or can even turn negative emotions into positives ones. This is achieved by looking at states, that is, what a person feels in a particular situation, including neurological activity, mental activity, physical energy, and emotions (Bossons, 2015). People often give these states names like *happy* or *relaxed*, and these names can be used to trigger complex unconscious processes within an individual. A leader can leverage this by inviting another person to first experience a state of positive arousal and then explore ways of getting to this state. The chemical reactions in remembering and reliving the state immediately change the other person's confidence.

LEADERS SUPPORTING AN ITERATIVE PROCESS

As a leader, you can support the confidence-building process by encouraging and guiding your followers: give them the time and space to do self-reflection and practice it yourself. Building confidence always starts with the individual. Then, invite others to join the reflection. Then, go back to self-reflection; this cycle is continuous. Over time, you and your people will have practiced *reflection with thinking and feeling* and will have developed your own approach to it, both as self-reflection and with peers.

This also supports a learning organization (Senge, 2006): every time it is practiced, the individual and the team are learning, tempering the effects of challenges and establishing a mutual support environment to get back to higher confidence levels.

APPLICATION IDEAS

Reflection by thinking and feeling must be experienced! In this section, you are invited to practice reflection so that you can then use it in your daily leadership work.

Application 1a:

Get Started: Experiencing *Reflection by Thinking and Feeling*

Many people come to know *reflection by thinking and feeling* by a short, 15-minute directed sequence. Take a piece of paper and a pen and look for a comfortable place where you can reflect for 15 minutes without being interrupted. Please respect this timeline, following them supports the power of reflection (Mueller, 2016).

1. *Please think about a current business-related challenge of yours. Write it down.* (Take 2 minutes.)
2. *Allow yourself a moment to feel if it already contains the core challenge – if not, rewrite it.* (Take 2 minutes.)
3. *Please **think** about the challenge and what you can do to solve it. Write down your thoughts.* (Take 3 minutes.)
4. *Now, please look at the **feelings** your challenge creates in your body.* (Take 2 minutes to feel and write down these feelings.)
5. *Now, imagine how it feels after the challenge has been solved.* (Allow yourself a minute to feel.)
6. *Please write down, in <u>one</u> word, how you would describe this state.* (Allow yourself a minute.)
7. *Please think about what you could do to reach this state.* (Take 2 minutes.)
8. *Write down what you have gained from this exercise.* (Take 2 minutes.)

Congratulations! You have mastered your first instance of *reflection by thinking and feeling*!

Application 1b:

Discovering the Gains From
Reflection by Thinking and Feeling

In our research, we have done this reflection with many leaders and managers around the world. We have grouped their gains in the table below. Please look at your notes from the reflection and tick all the items that apply to your experience:

Please select all items that describe your experience:

___ I have gained new perspectives or discovered new aspects related to my challenge.
___ I found more solutions or more creative solutions.
___ I found that the process of finding a solution became simpler.
___ I have gained a better understanding of my challenge.
___ I feel more relaxed about my challenge now than before the exercise.
___ I feel that my head, heart, and gut are better aligned.
___ None of the above applies to me.

Application 2:

Reflective Decision Making

Using reflection in decision making is a powerful tool, which we recommend in combination with the six steps of the decision quality model (see Figure 7.2) developed at Stanford (Spetzler, Winter, & Meyer, 2016):

Usually, this model is used in an analytical way by thinking about each chain link. This is suitable and leads to results. Adding feelings to the six steps develops decisions that are much more likely to be sustainable, as the people involved become much more committed.

Let us look closely at what happens within us when we use both thinking and feeling (see Figure 7.3).

If our head (thinking), heart (passion), and gut (feelings) are aligned when taking a decision, this decision will likely last and will be sustainable. It is important to note that alignment refers to a comfort band.

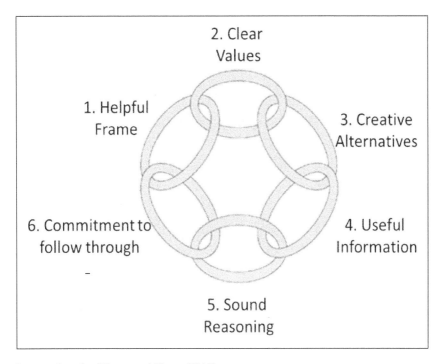

Source: Spetzler, Winter, and Meyer (2016).

Figure 7.2.   The decision quality model leads to good outcomes.

In cases were the head, heart, or gut are out of alignment, we can take decisions, but the energy level with which they will be implemented will be much lower than is possible, and their success is likely to be less sustainable.

When you work with people who are aligned, you can feel this: the energy level is much higher than usual, and it is gratifying to work together.

Application 3:

Develop a Reflection Habit

We recommend regular reflection at moments when you feel like doing so. This form shown in Figure 7.4 has proven useful to support this.

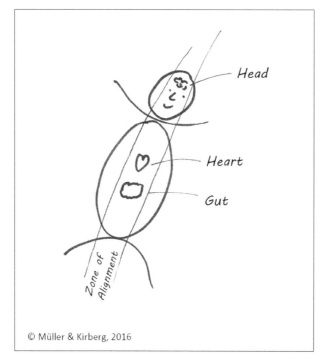

Figure 7.3.   The decision quality model leads to good outcomes.

Application 4:

Inviting Others to Experience *Reflection by Thinking and Feeling*

Guide your team through the reflection described before. As a leader, you can read the script and time the sections. Remember that a socioemotional environment is key to making reflection and learning happen.

Application 5:

Create a Relaxed Meeting Atmosphere

Meetings can be great moments of leadership. If you want to practice reflective leadership, the following sequence of events allows you to establish a socioemotional state in which all attendees can develop relationships of trust that contribute to the organization's goals:

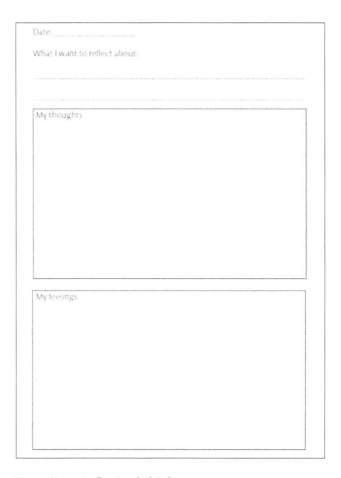

Figure 7.4.   Reflection habit form.

- Arrive relaxed: When approaching the meeting room, stop 20 meters before reaching it, take three deep breaths and then stroll in.
- Be mindful: The meeting is your key focus as long as it lasts. Turn off any distractions such as smartphones; only use your laptop or tablet to take notes or share files; don't check e-mails.
- Focus on relationships: Meetings are gatherings of people with the intention that being together and interacting add value. Thus, do not lose time sharing information; focus on interaction.
- Start with a story: Start the meeting in a relaxed manner by telling a story.

- Let everyone arrive: People have only fully arrived when they have spoken. Start your meeting with a check-in, where everyone says how they feel in one sentence. This includes you.
- 100% interaction: The highest usage of the people in the meeting is achieved if they engage in one-on-one relationships: 50% are sending and 50% are listening. Working in pairs is highly efficient and effective.

IMPLEMENTATION ADVICE

Most people intuitively understand, both intellectually and emotionally, the concepts behind reflective leadership and *reflection by thinking and feeling*. Many say that it seems natural and reminds them of how people are designed to be. Nonetheless, using *reflection by thinking and feeling* in our daily work requires us to change, which represents a challenge that may lead to stress and a drop in confidence.

As a leader, you can help build the confidence of those you lead so that they can move to this mode of operating with a few behaviors:

- **Practice what you preach:** When entering the world of feelings, people use different senses to assess a situation. They will easily detect if you are using reflective leadership from a place of conviction and commitment. Act as role-model. When giving them a few minutes in a meeting to gather their thoughts and feelings, do the same. Further, ensure that both they and you explicitly distinguish between feeling and thinking: from our upbringing, many of us respond by thinking when are asked about their feelings – you may want to consult some of the literature at the end of this chapter (Kline, 1999; Rosenberg, 2003).
- **Establish an environment conducive to** *reflection by thinking and feeling***:** As the fight-or-flight reaction can not be prevented in stressful situations, our brain has many operating modes that support or prevent certain activities. For learning, the brain has to move into the socioemotional operating mode. This mode is the natural default mode of brain operation, and allows us to access our own and others' feelings. The other, task-oriented mode is used for logical thinking and analysis and has become the default mode in business. Thus, ensure that you allow your people to move into the socioemotional mode. This is accomplished by creating an open atmosphere that is different from the situation in which we work on tasks—choose different locations and environments, break habits and hierarchies, and allow emotions to flow.

- **Do not replace stress with stress:** Acknowledging and talking about feelings is still an unusual activity in many societies and organizations today; this can lead to stress. Thus, while your intention may be to reduce stress caused by a challenge through reflective leadership, you do not want to replace one kind of stress with another. An effective way to deal with this is to introduce *reflection by thinking and feeling* on the go as part of everyday activities: Simply start a meeting by inviting each person to say one sentence about how they feel, and do not comment on this. By doing this and some of the other activities we have covered as you go, they become an accepted approach, and they allow your people to get acquainted with them and appreciate them.

- **Do not expect "traditional" results:** Traditionally, a leader is expected to produce results that are accomplished by the leader's actions. The success of meetings is measured by the number of items managed in a short time or the number of different topics managed by the leader. These traditional measures do not apply here: In reflective leadership, you lead by *nonaction*. Give yourself and them time and space; the process unfolds under your guidance. This is the biggest opportunity to be a leader; as Lao Tzu noted: "A leader is best when people barely know he exists, when his work is done, his aim fulfilled, they will say: we did it ourselves."

REFERENCES

Bandura, A. (1977). Self-efficacy: Toward a unifying theory of behavioural change. *Psychological Review, 84*(2), 191–215.

Bandura, A. (1994). Self-efficacy. In V. S. Ramachaudran (Ed.), *Encyclopedia of human behavior* (Vol. 4, pp. 71–81). New York, NY: Academic Press. (Reprinted in H.Friedman [Ed.], *Encyclopedia of mental health*. San Diego, CA: Academic Press, 1998).

Bandura, A. (2006). *Guide for creating self-efficacy scales.* In F. Pajares & T. C. Urdan, (Eds.), *Self-efficacy beliefs of adolescents* (pp. 307–338). Charlotte NC: Information Age.

Bossons, P., Riddell, P., & Sartain, D. (2015). *The neuroscience of leadership coaching.* London, England: Bloomsbury.

Boud, D., Keogh, R., & Walker, D. (1985). *Reflection: Turning experience into learning.* London, England: Kogan Page.

Confidence. (2016). *Merriam-Webster Online.* In Merriam-Webster. Retrieved January 1, 2016, from http://www.merriam-webster.com/dictionary/confidence

Damasio, A. (1994). *Descartes' error.* New York, NY: G.P. Putnam's Sons.

Damasio, A. (2000). *The feelings of what happens.* London, England: Random House.

Dewey, J. (1910). *How we think*. New York, NY: D.C. Heath & Company.

Goleman, D. (1996). *Emotional intelligence*. London, England: Bloomsbury.

Johns, C. (2009). *Becoming a reflective practitioner* (3rd ed.). Chichester, England: Wiley-Blackwell.

Kabat-Zinn, J. (2013). *Gesund durch Meditation* [Healthy through meditation]. München, Germany: Knaur.

Kahneman, D. (2011). *Thinking fast and slow*. New York, NY: Farrar, Straus and Giroux.

Kline, N. (1999). *Time to think*. London, England: Cassell Illustrated.

Lazarus, R., & Folkman, S. (1984). *Stress, appraisal and coping*. New York, NY: Springer.

Mueller, F. (2016). *An investigation into the role of thinking and feeling in increasing self-efficacy from within in doing business in a complex world*. Henley on Thames, England: Henley Business School.

Pajares, F. (1996). Self-Efficacy beliefs in academic settings. *Review of Educational Research, 66*(4), 543–578.

Rosenberg, M. (2003). *Nonviolent communication: A language of life*. Encinitas, CA: Puddle Dancer Press.

Senge, P. (2006). *The fifth discipline: The art & practice of the learning organization*. New York, NY: Doubleday.

Spetzler, C., Winter, H., & Meyer, J. (2016). *Decision quality: Value creation for better business decisions*. Hoboken, NJ: Wiley.

Stefano, G., Gino, F., & Pisano, G., & Staats, B. (2014). *Learning by thinking: How reflection aids performance*. Boston, MA: Harvard Business School.

CHAPTER 8

BLUE OCEAN LEADERSHIP AND WHY PSYCHOMETRIC TOOLS ARE STILL USEFUL TODAY

Wolfgang Amann

OBJECTIVE

This chapter deals with a recent innovation in the field of leadership as well as leadership development. It challenges some of the established assumptions. Blue ocean leadership introduces a sense of market realities to leadership behaviors and can therefore offer a powerful diverging framework and perspective. This chapter critically reviews what is behind the concept and outlines why psychometric tests still matter today.

MARKET REALITIES IN LEADERSHIP

Leadership is a concept that evolved drastically over the last 120 years. Around 1900, leaders were controllers. They observed in the face of emerging scientific management how efficiency could be maximized and output of any production facility increased. Employees were treated in a

Advanced Leadership Insights: How to Lead People and Organizations to Ultimate Success
pp. 101–105
Copyright © 2017 by Information Age Publishing

functional way akin to replaceable cogs in the wheel of efficient machines. Those were a time far from today's shifting focus to more sustainability, humanism and well-being in business. Around 1960, leadership shifted its focus toward the human relations. Happy workers are productive workers —or so the assumption went. Suddenly, there was more space to self-actualize through work. Staff engagement emerged as it was linked to better performance and more output. In this sense, the functional view on leadership as a means to an end had not fundamentally changed. Based on a plethora of tools created during World War II, psychometric tests and coaching attempted to provide personal insights and modify behavior, as long as it helped improve output. Leaders became therapists in a way. In the 1980s, the concept of transformational leadership gained in popularity. Beyond merely executing tasks, leaders were ought to improve systems while executing tasks. Leaders were encouraged to walk the talk, be inspirational, touch people's hearts and help their teammates grow. Roughly since 2007, the next wave within the leadership movement started. Eco-leadership spread as a concept. Attention shifted to follow us and situational requirements.

Blue ocean leadership (Kim & Mauborgne, 2014) falls into the category of eco-leadership, but adds unique innovations. The authors introduce the concept of market realities which made them famous within the field of strategizing. Blue ocean leadership addresses the question just how many colleagues and staff members are disengaged. The authors interpret disengagement as refusal to buy into the leadership behavior, which is offered to them. Around the world, disengagement ratios are high according to various studies, with more than two thirds of staff members in the West being disengaged, a percentage which reaches 90% in the Middle East and Northern Africa, and as high as 94% in East Asia, where scientific management, Taylorism and Fordism are still more popular (Kim & Mauborgne, 2014). Leaders cannot simply expect more performance from the rest of the organization through endless rounds of cost cutting, continuous improvement, mergers and acquisitions, digitalization strategies or international localization approaches. Kim and Mauborgne (2014) stress that leaders themselves have to step up. The following section explains how blue ocean leadership works.

DETAILING BLUE OCEAN LEADERSHIP

Blue ocean leadership breaks with the established tradition to start leadership or leadership development with personal qualities and behavioral styles. Instead of overemphasizing psychometric tests, such as MBTI, Firo B, Hogan, or LVI, leaders ought to engage staff members in more impactful small acts and activities. Based on discussions and negotiations, leaders and followers of blue ocean leadership agree on a leader's behavior which is more conducive for them. Similar to their concept, the authors suggest questions for negotiations with staff members:

1. What behaviors should a leader reduce?
2. What should a leader completely skip?
3. What should a leader do more of?
4. What should a leader add to his or her portfolio of behaviors in order to motivate, steer and engage staff members?

Leadership thereby becomes less generic and more connected to market realities. Leadership should no longer be overtly focused on the leader of the executives, but widen its scope to all managerial levels. The concept also calls for leadership as a task which does not require extra time. Leadership practices should be directly integrated in the regular activities to be carried out. There are some level specific lessons, although they have to be reviewed for the specific context of individual organizations. The authors, based on observations, suggest senior management to be less involved in the day-to-day operations and delegate more, while focusing on the company's future. Middle-management might have emphasized on control function, as well as risk management. However, middle managers henceforth should culture, liberate and empower more in order to set free a moral that creative energy is needed for innovation. Frontline managers, in turn are encouraged to attempt less to please the superiors and sharpen their intelligence in order to serve customers better, as they become empowered, liberated and coached.

WHY PSYCHOMETRIC TESTS
STILL MATTER NOW AND IN THE FUTURE

Blue ocean leadership represents a powerful tool for reflection on leadership. Are leaders actually effective if they create only disengaged staff members? This concept offers a unique moment of truth for the assessment of leaders. There are some fundamental lessons to be learned from it, especially when conceptual innovations are combined with traditional leadership and leadership development approaches.

To begin, it is correct that the work with psychometric tools is costly and time-consuming. It is frequently helpful to consult a coach to discuss the results of psychometric tests, plan steps ahead and review progress.

This is a costly process, no matter who pays for the tests as well as the coaches. Also, personality profiles reveal personal traits. It is important for leaders to develop self-awareness on their information processing, decision-making and execution preferences. The self-awareness can help leaders staff better and make better decisions. Going beyond self-awareness and exploring true leadership development, change needs time. Increasing one's leadership versatility, experimenting with innovations and critically reflecting upon them, can easily take up to one year. The timeframe might exceed the patience of disengaged staff members.

One area where the concept of blue ocean leadership might be overly pragmatic is the following. It might tempt leaders to skip the times much needed for personal development journey, if the focus is solely on the quick wins in the activities in the short-term. For example, introverts aspiring to be become chief executive officers have to learn how to be comfortable when speaking publicly. If a leader is aware of his or her limited repertoire of crisis management behaviors, there is benefit in polishing the required skills, although they might take time. In an ideal case, blue ocean leadership emerges with more traditional approaches. He or she learns how to trigger and sustain a midterm to long-term development journey based on psychometric tests, and if need be, coaching, while familiarizing oneself with the more pragmatic acts and activities to pull staff members out of disengagement.

This is essential because the negotiations and discussions leaders conduct with the staff members rely on the leader's emotional and social intelligence as well as the honed social skills. A broader leadership versatility can make negotiations on leadership innovations much more effective. Blue ocean leadership alone is therefore not enough.

If leaders ought to change the main foci, it is helpful to know more about their own predominant thinking styles and the alternatives that may exist. There is one more flaw or blind spot in the concept of blue ocean leadership. That staff members need to receive more attention is no longer a question. That staff members should have a voice, is more apparent now than before. There should be fair partnerships between leaders and their followers. There are moments, nevertheless, where leaders are expected to lead and even take unpopular decisions. Leaders need to obey highest ethical standards, which must be defended even if their decision becomes unpopular with staff members. The latter can then opt for not buying into the leadership behavior of their superiors, although this might occur due to the staff members not seeing the full picture. In addition, some change initiatives will not only produce winners and survivors—a phenomenon which can negatively affect popularity and engagement ratios. Occasionally, both the economic motor and logic of ensuring well-being for (surviving) staff members necessitate such change.

Leaders simply cannot be everyone's favorite at all times. This is an area underexplored in the concept of blue ocean leadership, although it is familiar to leaders and those actively engaged in leadership development.

SEMCO AS A CASE IN POINT

It is interesting to note that blue ocean leadership is not a conceptual framework alone. Long before business school professors "invented" it, there were inspiring examples brought to life in the real world. A case in point is Ricardo Semler at SEMCO in Brazil. He followed his father relatively early and took charge of the family business. Trying to be controlling and micromanaging, he failed and burned out. Instead of giving up, Semler changed his approach, and he introduced self-organization as a principle for organizing. He instructed the staff to organize in the way they preferred. Their pay, however, would be directly linked to their performance. Semler basically gave up control over those people that thoroughly knew the value creation process. Social dynamics ensured that latecomers were encouraged to be in time. Semler became famous for his concept of industrial democracy and corporate reengineering. His philosophy was not only applicable to the original mixer and agitator business he took over. He grew the company from its original USD 4 million in sales and created a diversified holding now worth USD 9.5 billion. His practices proved a later theory and its feasibility.

SUMMARY

This chapter outlines how to tackle one of today's most pressing challenges. Staff members around the world are disengaged. This can be interpreted as leaders truly being ineffective. While concepts, such as transformational leadership, have been around for more than two decades, they seem to be implemented with limited results. The concept of blue ocean leadership invites leaders to critically reflect upon the following questions to catalyze short-term results: which leadership behavior can you increase or decrease in order to be more impactful? Which leadership behaviors should you dismantle totally or which behaviors need to be formed in order to create more value?

REFERENCE

Kim, W., & Mauborgne, R. (2014). Blue ocean leadership: are your employees fully engaged in moving your company forward? Here's how to release their untapped talent and energy. *Harvard Business Review, 92*(5), 60–71.

PART III

LEADING THE ORGANIZATION TO ULTIMATE SUCCESS

CHAPTER 9

NAVIGATING COMPLEXITY

Ten Golden Principles
for CEOs Assuming Leadership

Katja Kruckeberg

OBJECTIVE

This chapter seeks to help newly appointed chief executive officers (CEOs) reflect on their priorities and making the best use of their time in their new role. The chapter focuses primarily on their first year, particularly on the first 100 days, since much of a newly appointed CEO's success is determined during this time. Based on our experience of working with CEOs across industries from around the world over the past 10 years, we propose 10 golden principles for new CEOs to reflect on when preparing for this next big step.

GOLDEN PRINCIPLE 1: DO YOUR HOMEWORK BEFORE YOU START

All CEOs we have worked with agree that their first year of tenure laid the foundation for their long-term success or, in a few cases, their long-term failure. However, the period before the new job starts is crucial and often

Advanced Leadership Insights: How to Lead People and Organizations to Ultimate Success
pp. 109–119

overlooked, although much can be accomplished during this time. Making the best of the time between their designation and the announcement can decide new CEOs' success or failure. This is when new CEOs still have a great deal of control over their time, but are not yet in the limelight. They can research information and can build relationships more freely. After the announcement, the various stakeholders' demands rise exponentially, and people change their attitudes toward a new CEO. Many CEOs we have spoken to regretted focusing too much on completing their old job, tying up loose ends, instead of preparing for their future challenges. Optimal use of this time depends on a number of factors that vary in each case. All new CEO must set their individual agenda for this time.

Topics to be addressed:

- Obtain your family's support;
- Prepare yourself mentally, emotionally, and physically;
- Learn about the company by talking to important stakeholders;
- Identify the key business challenges and opportunities;
- Assess your strengths and weaknesses in relation to the new role; and
- Prepare a story for Day 1.

If you are an internal hire, spend as much time with your predecessor as possible. What did this person do to monitor the company's health and progress? How did this CEO spend his or her time in the role? Where did this CEO focus his or her attention? What was this CEO's skills set and profile? Which activities did he or she value most and why?

Beyond needing to be aware that it is more important to use this time to prepare for the future than to complete your past, there is no formula to guide your focus in this time.

GOLDEN PRINCIPLE 2: FIND A SPARRING PARTNER

It is lonely at the top. You have probably heard this before. And while you will be dealing with more people than ever, the solitary nature of some of the major decisions you will need to make might be daunting. A sparring partner, whom you can use as a sounding board for your reflections, will be invaluable in such situations. Many CEOs we have worked with considered their spouse an important sparring partner and a source of emotional support. However, most CEOs relied on other confidants when wanting to talk business, for instance, their predecessor, a board member, high-ranking executives from other industries, and/or former school friends also in top management. In addition, many worked with executive coaches who helped them focus on what mattered, and advised them on building their management team and relationships with the company's key stakeholders. However, building a relationship with your predecessor can come at a price if he or she is still on the board. Such persons might support you, but might equally try to use you to push through their priorities.

GOLDEN PRINCIPLE 3: START WITH A MIXTURE OF CONFIDENCE AND HUMILITY

The biggest challenge is to start as you mean to carry on. It is a common mistake to think that you must have all the answers immediately. True, the pressure is on. You are in the limelight. Different stakeholders will try to pull you in different directions and pressure you into early long-term decision making. Resist this pressure. You will not yet have the knowledge, experience, or insights to make the best possible decisions at this time. Even if you already have the best answer, you need the most important people in the company's involvement, which will only happen once you have listened to their points of view.

However, you need to project confidence from day one and you need to have some kind of story ready for the people you talk to, without making promises you are unable to keep. This story could be partly about you (what you, as a leader, represents; what you believe in) and partly about the organization (e.g., the values you would like to instill in the organization, or how you want to (further) lead it to success). Experience suggests that you then have six to nine months to come up with the full picture of where you want the organization to go. Our recommendation is that you start by showing humility and showing your team, the organization, and the key stakeholders that you listen first in order to understand before you make decisions about the company's future. This is important when you come from inside the organization, but even more important if you come from the outside. First acknowledge the past and the present (achievements and failures) before you spell out the future. This gives you the opportunity to assess the organization's weaknesses and strengths, build relationships, and assess your potential. What weaknesses should you address and how?

GOLDEN PRINCIPLE 4: BUILD YOUR HIGH-PERFORMING TOP TEAM AS QUICKLY AS POSSIBLE

Research at Harvard Business School shows that the most successful CEOs are not necessarily the best decision makers or those with the most knowledge, but are often those with the ability to form high-performing teams to support them. Forming your top management team relatively quickly is critical for the company's performance. While you might have relied fairly successfully on your skills, expertise, and knowledge for quite some time, a CEO's success depends largely on having the right people beside him or her. You cannot run a company with an international presence on your own.

When you come from outside the organization, it is important to first get to know the people in your team, to assess and analyze their personality types before you take action. Interpersonal fit is at least as important as having the right capabilities on board. Identify people you can trust, and complete your team's skills set. If you are from the inside the organization, selecting and building your team can sometimes start before you are in the job. Our advice is that if you are sure you need to get rid of certain people, deal with this as soon as possible. An often overlooked alternative is to do this work with your predecessor. If you have the luxury to know about your designation months or even a year in advance, this could work. Two CEOs we have worked with had it all mapped out and had done all the work before he started! Either way, building your top team is a key priority during the first 100 days.

In Chapter 5, we introduced you to the *Five Success Factors of a High-Performing Team* pyramid (see Figure 9.1). We recommend that you use this approach, together with your management team, to agree on the framework of your cooperation. Only then can you grow, learn, and perform together most efficiently.

GOLDEN PRINCIPLE 5: SET THE BUSINESS AGENDA

How quickly you have to produce a new vision and a new strategic direction for your company (if you do have to) depends on your company's situation. However, a word of warning: We always suggest that you first know the company inside out before setting a new direction. Seventy percent of all major restructuring and change processes worldwide fail, mostly owing to the poor execution of the new strategy. You can lay a solid foundation for your business by improving its operations. If, during the first months, you spend a good proportion of your time with the people and the operation, you will get to know the company from different perspectives, which will lay the foundation for the new strategic direction. Short-term thinking and long-term thinking must be in balance from day one. You must have a clear idea of where you want to go before you start moving: be sure that you know what the key business issues were in the past and the challenges and opportunities that others foresee in the future before setting

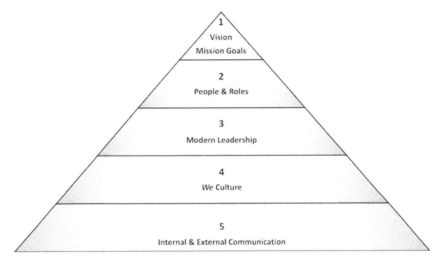

Figure 9.1.   The Five Success Factors of a High-Performing Team pyramid.

out a new direction. The most successful CEOs we have worked with spent their first 3 months listening to the organization to avoid the trap of jumping to conclusions too early. In the process, they had to make deliberate decisions about whom to listen to and which questions to ask.

One CEO decided to talk to the 50 most important managers in the company, including all the board members. He sent them these questions and asked them to give their opinions within a certain time frame:

- Which three things must we hold on to?
- Which three things must we change?
- What do you hope I will do as a CEO?
- What advice do you have for me?

After receiving their written answers, he reached out to everyone to discuss their answers in depth and to get to know them better, also at a more personal level. Another executive made it his goal to, in the first 3 months, talk to all the board members, the 10 most important customers, the 10 most important shareholders, the 10 most important regional leaders, the 10 most important managers, the 10 most important people on the shop floor, and so forth, to get to know their views of the company and how they saw its future direction.

Whichever approach you take to be fully informed, experience shows that the new strategic positioning should then follow within the first 6 to 9 months of your tenure. It takes confidence to not make any immediate decisions, as everyone around you will be watching you closely; in most cases, however, it is better to resist the pressure. Our golden advice from the CEOs we work with is: first understand, then plan, and then implement. And when you start implementing changes, involve the people in your organization, the key stakeholders outside the organization, and your customers. Remember, it destroys value if your focus as a CEO, is too introspective and you forget about the organization's customers.

GOLDEN PRINCIPLE 6: DEFINE THE CORPORATE CULTURE

Cultural intervention should be an early priority of every CEO. This intervention clarifies what your company is capable of, even as you refine your strategy. Coherence between your culture, strategic direction, and performance goals can make your organization more appealing to both employees and customers. According to Jon R. Katzenbach's (Katzenback, Steffen, & Kronley, 2012) work, which many of our clients have used to initiate a cultural change that suited their company best, you should be aware of the following aspects before initiating and implementing cultural change in your company.

Match Strategy and Culture

All too often, a company's strategy imposed from above is at odds with the ingrained practices and attitudes of its culture. Executives may underestimate how much a strategy's effectiveness depends on its cultural alignment. Culture trumps strategy every time (Katzenbach et al., 2012).

Focus on a Few Critical Shifts in Behavior

Studies show that only 10% of people who have had heart surgery subsequently make major modifications to their lifestyles. We tend to not change our behavior, even in the face of overwhelming evidence. Therefore, choose your battles: if a few key behaviors are strongly emphasized, employees will often develop additional ways to reinforce them (Katzenbach et al., 2012).

Honor the Strengths of Your Existing Culture

It is tempting to focus on your culture's negative aspects, but any corporate culture will have many strengths. Acknowledging the existing culture's benefits will also make major change feel less like a top-down activity and more like a shared evolution (Katzenbach et al., 2012).

Integrate Formal and Informal Interventions

As you emphasize new key behaviors, make people aware how they affect the company's strategic performance and integrate formal approaches (e.g., new rules, metrics, and incentives) with informal interactions (behavior modeling by senior leaders, peer-to-peer interactions, storytelling, engagement of motivational leaders, changes to the premises, resources, and aesthetics) (Katzenbach et al., 2012).

Measure and Monitor a Cultural Evolution

Finally, it is important, as one would do with any other high-priority business initiative, to measure and monitor the cultural progress at each stage of your efforts. Rigorous measurement allows executives to identify backsliding, to correct the course where needed, and to demonstrate tangible evidence of improvement, which can help maintain positive momentum over the long haul (Katzenbach et al., 2012).

GOLDEN PRINCIPLE 7: MANAGE YOUR STAKEHOLDERS

Every CEO has a number of important stakeholders to deal with. Get to know the individual board members as soon as possible. Most of the CEOs we have worked with and whose interviews we have analyzed mention that it is important to spend time with these people, inside and outside the organization. Try to understand their personality types and put yourself in their shoes. They each have a different perspective on how the organization should be taken forward. Get to know all these different perspectives. In addition, there is often a board within the board, an inner circle of power. Try to find out who plays which role.

A simple technique that many CEOs use to manage their stakeholders effectively is to draw a mind-map. Put yourself at the center. Place all the important stakeholders you are dealing with around you: Your board, the employees, your management team, your customers, distributors, industrial partners, media, politicians, and so on. Identify the most important people in these stakeholder groups—people whom you can trust to deliver. As a CEO, you need to be aware of all of these people all the time. Trust and transparency are keywords when managing these relationships.

GOLDEN PRINCIPLE 8: COMMUNICATE DELIBERATELY

As a new leader, one of your key responsibility is to effectively manage your communication with all the relevant different stakeholders. We urge you to produce a clear communication plan early on in your new role. Work on and adapt this plan continuously. The content of your communication is as important as how you communicate. As human beings, we communicate verbally and nonverbally all the time, whether or not we intend to; consequently, your communication must become more deliberate. Everything you do will be under scrutiny—you are like a rock star whose every move is watched. When you arrive at work, the car you drive, the clothes you wear, the jokes you tell … everything you do matters.

You also need to think carefully about the means of communication you choose for your message and how you can build an image of yourself as an excellent communicator. A key activity in this respect is to work on your leadership presence (see Figure 9.2).

You will find more information on how to build your leadership presence and become a more charismatic communicator in Chapter 2.

GOLDEN PRINCIPLE 9: MANAGE YOUR ENERGY SUSTAINABLY

Managing your energy is a critical task for a CEO. It is going to be a challenging time emotionally, mentally, physically, socially and, in some ways, even spiritually. You will soon not only feel like a corporate citizen, but also like a corporate athlete. Manage your resources and energy sustainably, or run the risk of paying the price sooner than you may think. Almost all the CEOs we know who have succeeded in doing so, took this task of finding a balance seriously. Many made an effort to spend enough time with their families, since a good work-life balance can be the key to overall wellbeing. Having said this, it's no secret that the job is very time-intensive. Spending quality time with your family, switching off from work, and being fully present with the people you care for most can make all the difference. Healthy eating and regular exercise should be part of every busy CEO's toolkit. If you neglect your overall wellbeing, the pressure can become too much.

GOLDEN PRINCIPLE 10:
BROADEN YOUR LEADERSHIP CAPABILITIES CONTINUOUSLY

The best CEOs we have come across had one outstanding quality: they learned more quickly and more consciously than others. They continu-

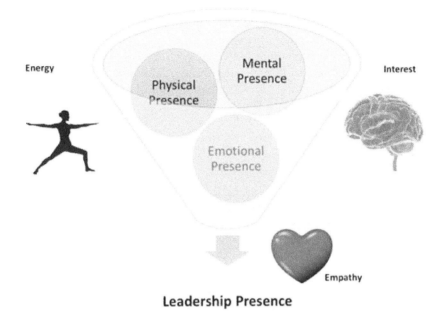

Figure 9.2.   Three levels of your leadership presence.

ously made an effort to develop themselves further, because they knew that what had taken them to one career position would not be enough to get them to the next one. They understood that, during each leadership transition, they had to adopt a new mindset, to polish their leadership and management skills, and to spend their time at work differently (with a larger set of different stakeholders).

Mindset

As a new CEO, you need to develop a CEO mindset quickly. For instance, if you were a chief financial officer previously, you might have primarily focused on costs, but, as a new CEO, your focus will probably need to switch to revenues. You might need to start looking for products and portfolios, and you might realize that you need to develop a more holistic approach than the one you had previously. Innovation and change management might be new activities for you. Regardless of the career path that led you to this new challenge, you need to start thinking more holistically and comprehensively to succeed in your new post.

Leadership Skills

There are various leadership concepts that team leaders can use to polish their leadership capabilities. We suggest the concept based on the work of Daniel Goleman (2000), who became famous with his bestselling book on emotional intelligence. Goleman differentiates between six leadership styles, which we briefly describe in Table 9.1.

In Chapter 6, you will find a diagnostic tool that can help you assess your current leadership practice and can provide ideas on how to develop yourself further.

Time Application

Every leadership transition brings a new set of task and challenges. You can deal with these successfully by spending your time more deliberately

Table 9.1.   Six Leadership Style

Directive Leadership Style	*Visionary Leadership Style*	*Affiliative Leadership Style*
This *do what I say* approach can be very effective in a turnaround situation, a natural disaster, or when working with challenging employees. If over-used, a commanding leadership blocks the organization's flexibility and diminishes employee motivation.	A visionary leader takes a *come with me* approach: He or she states the overall goals, yet gives people the freedom to choose their own ways to achieve results. This style works especially well when a business is in a difficult situation. It is less effective when the leader works with an expert team more experienced than the leader.	The affiliative leader has a *people come first* attitude. This style is particularly useful for building team harmony or increasing morale. But its exclusive focus on praise can allow poor performance to go uncorrected. The affiliative leader rarely offers direct feedback or advice, and thus leaves employees unclear about their performance.
Democratic Leadership Style	*Pace-Setting Leadership Style*	*Coaching Leadership Style*
By giving workers a voice in decisions, democratic leaders build organizational flexibility and responsibility, and help generate fresh ideas. Sometimes the price is endless meetings and confused employees who feel underled. There is a positive impact on the organizational climate, but not as high as one might imagine.	A leader who sets high performance standards and exemplifies them, has a positive impact on highly competent and self-motivated employees. However, others may feel overwhelmed by the continual demand for strong results and high standards; some will resent this leader's tendency to take over.	This style focuses more on personal development than on immediate work-related tasks. It works well when employees are already aware of their weaknesses and want to improve, but not when they are resistant to changing their ways.

focusing on the topics that matter most. The day only has 24 hours, which means that CEOs must quickly learn how to best use their time. Our recommendation is to discuss these issues with other seasoned businesspeople. Time is your most valuable resource, and you need to spend it well.

RESOURCES

Coyne, K. P., & Rao, B. S. Y. (2005). A guide for the new CEO elect. *McKinsey Quarterly*. Retrieved from http://www.mckinsey.com/global-themes/leadership/a-guide-for-the-ceo-elect

Favaro, K., Karlsson, P.-O., & Neilson, G. L (2012). *Navigating the first year: Advice from 18 chief executives*. Retrieved from http://www.strategy-business.com

Goleman, D. (2000). Leadership that gets results. *Harvard Business Review*. Retrieved from https://hbr.org/2000/03/leadership-that-gets-results

Katzenbach, J. R., Steffen, I., & Kronley, C. (2012). Cultural change that sticks. *Harvard Business Review*. Retrieved from https://hbr.org/2012/07/cultural-change-that-sticks

Neff, T., & Citrin, J. (2016). *Now you're in charge: the first 100 days*. Retrieved from https://www.spencerstuart.com

Torres, R., & Tollmann, P. (2012). *Mythen der ersten 100 Tage* [Myths of the first 100 days]. Retrieved from www.harvardbusinessmanager.de

CHAPTER 10

STAKEHOLDER MANAGEMENT AS A LEADERSHIP CHALLENGE

Wolfgang Amann

OBJECTIVE

This chapter outlines one of the surprises that await leaders at the higher levels. While leaders are able to rely on formal, disciplinary power to lead subordinates, their reality changes higher up in the career ladder. Leaders ought to manage stakeholders effectively as a sign of being a great leader. Thus, reflecting on how to leverage stakeholders and stakeholder management represents a worthwhile endeavor if a leader wants to create ultimate success.

MCDONALD'S IN ARGENTINA AS A CASE IN POINT

A few years ago, the chief executive officer (CEO) of McDonald's was confronted with a challenging situation. A woman claimed to have eaten in one of the restaurants, and fallen sick immediately afterwards for which she accused McDonald's. The health authorities shut down a few restaurants and threatened to close down more facilities. Local politicians began paying attention to the issue, as they (mis)used the situation to mobilize publicity for themselves before the upcoming election. Politicians had the

Advanced Leadership Insights: How to Lead People and Organizations to Ultimate Success
pp. 121–125
Copyright © 2017 by Information Age Publishing
All rights of reproduction in any form reserved.

choice of either lambasting the capitalist foreign company, for not paying attention to health factors, or they could side with McDonald's as the largest private employer in the country, to possibly secure more jobs. Parents became concerned whether they should visit McDonald's as a "family place" to eat. Staff members were concerned whether job security. Headquarter began wondering if the management and leadership in place was truly effective in handling the situation. There were a few provisions in place to prepare leaders accordingly. Lastly, but certainly not the least, journalists jumped on the issue, as negative news cultivated sensationalism and fostered sales. There was an opportune moment for investigative journalists to build a reputation for themselves during such a commotion. The CEO in place was probably and involuntarily stuck in a situation characterized by the ultimate time pressure. He knew that the company's hygienic standards were competitive. Scientific tests on the bacteria would take more time, which he did not have. What could he say in a forthcoming town hall meeting to the stakeholders assembled? Was denial an option? Could he condemn the sick woman in the hospital? Could she side with politicians? How would he handle the health authority representatives? What commitments should be made? What messages did he have for all of the different stakeholders?

ON DIPLOMACY AND STAKEHOLDER MANAGEMENT SKILLS

The McDonald's Argentina case is one of the examples we use in our leadership development courses to prepare current and future leaders for challenging tasks. Neither in real life, and nor in the classrooms there is enough time to conjure up the perfect answer. Hence, it is essential that leaders clarify the very values they stand for. It is of equal importance that leaders proactively develop their stakeholder management skills. Leaders at higher levels must master self-management skills, the ability to function and create value through others, integrating value across silos, units, and functions, trigger system change within the organization, but also, as outlined above in the example of McDonald's, leaders must manage stakeholders. Figure 10.1, based on Amann, Khan, Salzmann, Steger, and Ionescu-Somers (2007), outlines overall options. When confronted with external pressure, which could be higher or lower, leaders need to make a choice about how they should react to that pressure. They can have a softer or harder attitude, leaving a leader with a classic 2 × 2 matrix for the decision-making. The "nice guy" is probably the most preferred attitude of all. The company may be generous, come across as friendly and build relationships proactively. "Stealth bomber" behavior is often a necessity. Donald Trump was known during his businessmen days to immediately send an army of lawyers and

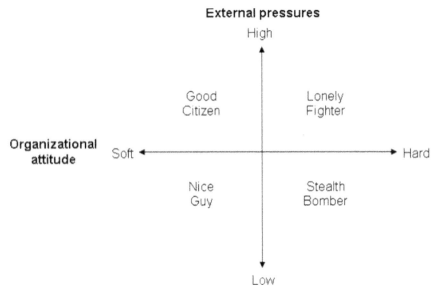

Figure 10.1.   Corporate diplomacy options for stakeholder management

threatened with lawsuits if he did not get his will. Such measures build little social capital for the future and for times when leaders and organizations have to rely on public goodwill.

McDonald's is a different situation in the above mentioned case. There was substantial external pressure from all directions. The CEO has to decide whether to adopt a "good citizen" or "lonely fighter" attitude against all positions. In our research as well as coaching work with executives, we encourage good corporate citizenship for number of reasons. First, society expects companies to be bendable and players (in return of the opportunity to receive profits from society). Second, well-being should be the final goal of business activities, and if there are wrongdoings or risks, there is no need to create additional problems through fights. Third, stakeholders in the above mentioned case did not want to see denial or a CEO attempting to appear full of integrity. They demanded answers. They expected a real dialog, not just a debate. There is a stark difference between the two concepts. Stakeholder debate may create winners and losers, which are often lead with an egocentric attitude. They focus on talking at others or influencing stakeholders. In contrast, a stakeholder dialog targets the following:

- cooperation in order to achieve consensus on both the right procedures as well as outcomes;

- true empathy where one party sincerely attempts to understand others;
- authenticity in the sense of not selling a manipulative corporate image;
- talking with and listening to others;
- convincing with the best arguments, not power-selling;
- adopting a constructive mindset and allocating most of the energy on solving problems, not playing the blame game;
- admitting own vulnerability in creating transparency on interests;
- working toward shared responsibilities, not distracting; and
- intentionally avoiding delays or complicating solutions as tactics.

The CEO at McDonald's Argentina managed to convince the stakeholders that he will take care of the situation, carry out thorough tests, and guarantee jobs and health standards while forgoing some profits. He also triggered some midterm changes in the company's global crisis policies as likelihood exists that such crisis situations will reemerge elsewhere. The CEO knew something was not right with the claims of the "victim." The bacteria which allegedly had infected the woman, needed a longer incubation period to cause harm. It was soon revealed that she was running a scam. She went from industry to industry accusing companies to have caused her suffering, in order to extort money. As industries do not frequently communicate with each other, she had gotten away with the swindle for quite some time.

SUMMARY

Stakeholder management represents one of the foundational skills for high-level leaders. It is reasonable to expect that crisis will emerge in the timeline of one's leadership tenure. The question we invite the reader to reflect upon is the following: to what extent have you prepared yourself for crisis management? To what extent are solutions ready and provided by the company? To what extent do you feel comfortable coming to the office not being able to work on the planned activities but managing tough crises as the one outlined above? It gets lonelier at the top. Competitors from within and outside the company wait for a leader to make a mistake. Yet, true leaders mentally prepare for such situations and these expectations. They embrace adversity, instead of shying away from it. True leaders accept reality and the likelihood of unseen crises materializing, they do not deny that anything could happen to them.

REFERENCE

Amann, W., Khan, S., Salzmann, O., Steger, U., & Ionescu-Somers, A. (2007). Managing external pressures through corporate diplomacy. *Journal of General Management, 33*(1), 33–50.

CHAPTER 11

WOMEN IN LEADERSHIP

Aspirations, Obstacles, and Opportunities

Ruth Ann Lake and Cristina Bombelli

OBJECTIVE

In this chapter we see that men's and women's leadership ambitions are the same. However, countries lose gross national product output owing to lower participation by women in their workforce as productivity rankings are higher for companies with greater diversity. Leadership styles typical of women leaders are more suited to younger generations.

LEADERSHIP AMBITIONS

Research shows that women express the same if not a greater desire to be in leadership positions than men, although they often ask for more training and support. In spite of this, most companies across the developed world have very few female managers in their leadership pipeline, and this situation is changing only incrementally. In the latest Organisation for Economic Co-operation and Development (OECD) report, less than one third of senior management positions are occupied by women, and the OECD pay gap remains at around 15.5% (OECD Data, 2013).

Advanced Leadership Insights: How to Lead People and Organizations to Ultimate Success
pp. 127–142

In its recent 2015 report, *Women Matter*, McKinsey claimed that $12 trillion could be added to global gross national product output by 2025 if there were full utilization of women's talents in countries' workforces. Social and cultural factors are such that even where legislation speaks of equal pay for equal work, wage gaps persist, and without any incentives to realize the goals of greater equality, it is widely predicted that "natural" progress, with things left as they are, would take more than 100 to 150 years (McKinsey, 2015a).

Companies with greater diversity in their leadership ranks outperform traditional enterprises; thus, an economic incentive would call for compliance with goals of diversity, reflecting the client communities and the communities in which companies are based. While some women, driven to rise to the top, feel compelled to imitate male models, crashing through the glass ceiling via brute force by adopting aggressive and competitive behaviors, authentic leadership calls on people to be truly themselves and to practice their own unique leadership style, remembering to look over their shoulders to note whether in fact there are followers—the sine qua non definition of being a leader.

Research from Wise Growth (2015), a Milan-based consultancy, also shows that women leaders are more attuned to social and personalized rewards types and apparently use a leadership style more akin to that considered desirable to the new generations entering the workforce. It would generally appear that women are more motivated by personalized and nonmonetary intrinsic rewards than strictly monetary and other traditional rewards such as the status of having a big office, et cetera (see Figure 11.1).

- For men, promotions are based on potential; for women, promotions are based on their track records.
- Despite advances in higher education, a confidence gap persists among women.
- Women are judged more harshly for self-promotion than men.
- Women are locked out of many networks needed to "climb the ladder."

To support and help prepare this generation of women leaders, companies need to be aware of their requests for greater support and training. There is often a *confidence gap* that stems from socialization issues, not from any significantly different level of formal preparation or years of experience. In fact, in most developed countries, women are now graduating from universities in greater proportional numbers than men. Despite this, women tend to enroll in more humanistic specializations and often

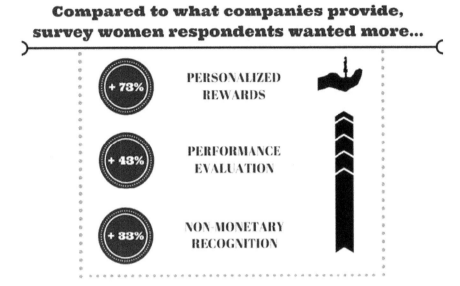

Compared to what companies provide, survey women respondents wanted more...

+ 73% PERSONALIZED REWARDS

+ 43% PERFORMANCE EVALUATION

+ 33% NON-MONETARY RECOGNITION

Figure 11.1.   Companies are not meeting women's needs for development.

remain the minority in engineering or in the advanced sciences and mathematics. While tests reveal that girls and boys have similar abilities in math and science in primary schools, by the time children reach adolescence, a significant *math anxiety* disproportionately affects female students. Other studies have shown that, whether true or not, many prepubescent girls perceive that it is more socially acceptable in their secondary schools to excel in languages or the humanities than in science or math, particularly when trying to gain popularity and success in their social circles. One study showed that boys are less likely to date a girl who excels in science or math or who outperforms him in the sports arena, thus inducing a social phobia type of being labeled a *nerd* and therefore being marginalized. Studies also show that girls and women need more encouragement and mentorship to help overcome the confidence gap fueled by ubiquitous comments about the mismatch between being female and going into mathematical, technical, or scientific fields (McKinsey 2015b).

While girls and women may need more encouragement, boys and men, who are raised in competitive environments, tend to show more willingness to rise to new challenges with a certain boldness. Research has shown that *men are often promoted based on perceptions of their potential, while women get promoted based on their track records and achievements* (Mohr, 2014). It is more typical for a male candidate to put forward his résumé for a new position even if he only meets 60% of the listed requirements, while women normally wait until they are at close to the 95% level. Men also seem to have a more developed sense of working *old boys networks*, tending to stay after a formal meeting to develop contacts and to find out what is happening in the company, while women tend to dash off to the next meeting, trying to cram in as many decisions as possible during the work day and trying to leave the office on time to take care of family priorities. Women are less comfortable dealing with *office or power politics*. While wielding power and influence is part of the way things work in many organizations, women often seem more focused on the "dark side" of power, and are more reluctant to draw on behaviors that exhibit command and power for fear of being labeled as "bossy" or "aggressive," often accompanied with negative connotations when the actors are female. Women are also more typically the designated parent for doing school runs or being present in early evenings to help with children's or family activities.

CONTINUED INEQUALITY ON THE HOME FRONT

While there has been some progress toward more women in middle management, inequality at home remains entrenched, with women dedicating considerably more hours to managing children, the household, caring for elderly relatives, and including her male partner's parents. These tasks create a heavy workload for an upwardly mobile woman and generate considerable stress and distress. The North European countries have made more progress on this front, while Southern Europe, particularly countries such as Italy and Greece, lag far behind. A McKinsey study (2015a) found that the path to leadership is disproportionately stressful for women owing to these and other factors.

THE OBSTACLES FOR WOMEN IN FINDING THE DELICATE BALANCE BETWEEN VISIBILITY AND APPEARING BRASH

It is more typical for men to "blow their own horns" when speaking of their achievements, successful projects and results; doing so can often help to create a personal leadership brand of a confident person who is fully capable of taking on a new project or career opportunity. When one study asked people to read "boastful statements," if the comments went too far, the speaker was considered arrogant; yet if the speaker were identified as female, the disapproval rate was 42% higher than that attributed to men. The women speakers' *likeability* declined dramatically. In an infamous study done at Harvard and cited in Sheryl Sandberg's (2013) book *Lean In*, the name of a successful entrepreneur in an identical business case study was Howard to half the students and to Heidi to the other half. At the end of the case study, the students were asked if they would like to work for Howard or Heidi. Both candidates were ranked as equally competent, but Heidi was perceived as somewhat "egotistical, a bit political"; thus, the respondents stated they would prefer *not* to work for her. On the other hand, both men and women students thought it would be interesting to work for Howard, who was perceived to be a "good leader." The researchers' result was that success and likability were positively correlated for men leaders and negatively correlated for females (Heilman & Okimoto, 2007).

To create a more favorable environment for the develop of young females in organizations and to supply the pipeline with future talent, the human resource (HR) function should consider the enactment of policies that are more gender neutral or less compromising for some actors such as female workers and leaders.

CHANGE THE WAYS RECRUITMENT AND HIGH POTENTIAL INDUCTION WORK

Given that most young graduates today cannot hope to enter a company at a professional level unless they have a master's degree, the entry age is moving back to the mid to late 20s. Even in recruitment, studies show that interviewers often assume that female candidates will soon be pregnant and wanting to stay home, while with men they do not have this concern. The consequences are often fewer opportunities for women first entering professional jobs.

HIGH POTENTIAL PROGRAMS OFTEN TARGET YOUNG TALENT IN THEIR 30S, THE BEST AGE BRACKET FOR SUCCESSFUL CHILD-BEARING

High potential programs aimed at developing male and female talent often create a list of potential candidates, who then become eligible for special training, mentoring, coaching, and other advantages of being in an "elite" group. The drawing up of lists often includes those in their 30s and coincides with the typical child-bearing years of women with advanced university studies. This forces a difficult choice for many, between their career or starting a family life with children. Men can opt to put off fatherhood into their early 40s with few consequences on their ability to have a family some day. Women do not have this option; to ease distress, a handful of employers, such as Facebook and Apple, have begun to expand their healthcare plans to allow women, if they to choose to do so, to freeze their eggs, so they can have a better chance of maternity later on than would otherwise be available. These policies are somewhat controversial, but expand the options for employees and at least provides a right to choose such an option. In most companies, women do not have this option, so a decision is effectively forced on them; constraints force them to sacrifice one of their two desired objectives.

Companies looking to mitigate this effect would do well to expand their pool of "high potentials" to include individuals into their mid 40s, to attempt to consider factors of gender and other diversity as a key part of their selection process.

MANAGEMENT OF PARENTAL LEAVE

Upon entry into the organizational environment, HR policies can help or hinder the advancement of female talent up the leadership path. A specific corporate culture may well determine how effective written policies are in practice. Cultural obstacles persist, resulting in different usage levels, for instance of parental leave policies in environments with larger cultural acceptance of the same. Many men and women perceive that if they fully utilize the benefits offered by their organizations, they will somehow be penalized. In the cited McKinsey (2015a) study, up to 90% of respondents (both men and women) in the United States feared being penalized if they took extended family leave. In the Nordic countries, fathers taking leave has gradually gained more social acceptance; thus, the percentage of new fathers that take family leave has steadily increased.

WHERE FATHERS TAKE PATERNITY LEAVE, ALL INDICATORS FOR FEMALE PARTICIPATION ARE HIGHER

The Economist publishes a Glass Ceiling Index every year on March 8—International Women's Day. In the 2016 edition, it included new parental leave criteria, also including the statistics on where new fathers have the right to and actually take leave. There is a positive correlation between places where men take leave and women's participation in the labor market, female employment generally, and a lower gap in salary differences between men and women. The Nordic countries came out on top, with Norway, Sweden, and Finland in the lead (*The Economist,* 2016).

WOMEN STILL TEND TO GRAVITATE TOWARD STAFF RATHER THAN LINE POSITIONS, LIMITING ASCENT UP THE LADDER

Even in countries where women are more represented in management, they tend to gravitate to staff and support functions such as HR, public relations, administration, and finance rather than to line positions from which candidates are frequently recruited into senior positions. The same underlying reasons are often the basis for the choice. These positions generally call for less travel and are often less onerous in terms of overtime or extras such as dealing with client emergencies or production shutdowns, which falls to the technical departments, which are more typically dominated by male managers. Often, the reason is that women are choosing a career type that more easily fits with the desire to spend significant time with their family rather than rushing off around the world to fix problems or spending weekends at the factory dealing with technical crises. It is often their perception and that of their male partner in that, where children are concerned, women are at the front line in case of illness, management of weekly activities such as music lessons, sports, scouting, other activities, and dealing with school-related and health-related issues. Women are choosing to have balance in their lives and to treasure time spent on personal objectives and family. There is often little desire to emulate or delve into the traditional model of being "married to the company" and sliding into the workaholic behaviors that are often perceived as a prerequisite for gaining advancement in the organization. Indeed, younger men and women are also much less interested in spending their lives at the office or being contactable 24/7, and wish to dedicate time to their personal objectives and family life.

THE QUEST FOR BALANCE

Organizations can boost the numbers of women in middle and upper management by demonstrating that new mothers and fathers are not discriminated against, that they are just as eligible to be assigned to interesting projects and to be considered for promotions. If this is not the case, the "writing is on the wall," and the statistics will reflect the reality in the company's hallways, rather than the texts buried in HR files. Many fathers, especially from younger generations, approach fatherhood from a totally different perspective than their fathers did via the "traditional breadwinner" approach. They want to be present in the lives of their children and their family, and are likely to balk at the unwritten rules requiring overtime, weekend e-mailing, and phone calls that most if not all corporations now take for granted. In recent years, companies have become aware that some—desirable—candidates check potential employ-

Figure 11.2.   What does it take for companies to develop a better leadership pipeline for women?

ers' rankings on the *family-friendly indices*, now widely available in developed countries.

TRAINING, COACHING, AND MENTORING OPPORTUNITIES

Wise Growth (2015) research shows that women, more so than male employees, perceive the need for greater organizational support (see Figure 11.2).

CONTENT OF TRAINING PROGRAMS
FOR DEVELOPING WOMEN IN LEADERSHIP

To counter these tendencies and obstacles, companies can develop more women leaders in their pipeline by sponsoring workshops and coaching programs aimed at:

- helping women to identify and act on the confidence gap;
- developing more accurate awareness of one's competencies, strengths, and skills gaps;

- encouraging women to speak up and develop the skills and courage to put themselves forward for new projects and positions;
- helping women in organizations to understand the dynamics of power and to learn influencing skills essential to more effectively engage people both inside and outside the organization, as well as to more effectively manage their career trajectory;
- learning how to develop one's own path to leadership rather than copy the predominant male models in the public eye;
- acquire the skills and techniques to effectively manage the female tendency toward perfectionism and to manage stress;
- provide tools to analyze one's work-life balance and how to reach equilibrium;
- exploring how an organizational culture can more effectively meet the motivational needs of male and female actors so as to maximize performance and motivation; and
- working to overcome barriers to participation in existing programs to allow parental leave and ensuring that, whether male of female, those who choose to participate do not suffer career obstacles or are not penalized in terms of being exclusion from interesting projects.

AWARENESS OF INTERNAL BARRIERS AND DEVELOPING PATHS TO MINIMIZE SELF-LIMITING BEHAVIORS

A key part of the work to minimize the confidence gap involves developing awareness on the many self-limiting behaviors common to women in the workforce. Women often develop the habit of sitting on the sidelines, speaking up less than men in meetings, avoiding opposing another's ideas in a confrontational setting, of being or becoming less visible in the eyes of the department or team. In every family and every culture, there are different—often very subtle—forces that socialize women to play a more modest role, to avoid self-promotion, and to seek cooperation and harmony. While these are not negative traits, they can limit women to taking a back seat in organizational life, retreating from the often inevitable battles for scarce resources and simply not offering themselves as protagonists or candidates for exciting and sometimes risky lead roles in high-profile projects. There is a belief that hard work alone will be recognized (by someone else), and that this will eventually lead to a greater professional opportunity. Indeed, many successful women owe their promotions or opportunities to sponsors or advocates (often men in senior positions) who backed them for positions. The same can happen for male candidates, but what distinguishes many female candidates is their humility or lack of assertiveness in putting themselves forward and almost being taken by surprise when nominated by someone else. Wise Growth (2015) has identified this phenomenon as the "accidental manager"; it is common among successful career women (Bombelli 2009). When a promotion is granted and a new position taken up, many women attribute this to luck —being at the right place at the right time and having met the right person, who put their name forward. Men more often attribute promotion to their own inherent qualities and achievements. Thus, women need to learn to speak up more, to ask for the next opportunity, in a way that is coherent with their personality, their expertise, and the professional sector.

DEVELOPING APPLIED ASSERTIVENESS

In some workshops aimed at developing women leaders, assertiveness is addressed; beyond theoretical and or conceptual models, practice and feedback are useful. The first step is often to build awareness of their actual assertiveness level, or lack thereof. Many women employees and managers may be opposed to separate training or coaching opportunities for female potentials, considering it a type of *reverse discrimination*. There is often very low awareness of the subtle factors in many societies and cultures that tend to create situations in which women simply do not speak up as often as men in meetings and during critical decision-making moments. Techniques involving the use of short films and company-specific case studies can create opportunities for sharing ideas and can allow participants to identify their internal blockers, which are often in the shadow of their awareness.

PRACTICING ASSERTIVE COMMUNICATION

Beyond awareness, it is often useful to create a *safe space* in a workshop to allow women to practice a dialogue they intend to have with an individual in their company, perhaps an elevator pitch to a potential sponsor, a line to introduce an important presentation, or a request to be communicated prior to an upcoming meeting. Often, the choice of words, tone, and body language create an impression of a lack of assertiveness, much to the chagrin of the female team leader or manager, who does not intentionally want to project this. Individuals should be helped to assess the impacts of the messages they are creating and to decide where to tweak them or tone them up or down. Facilitators can enlist colleagues to provide qualified feedback; often, there is valuable learning and some ready-made tools or "ammunition" to bolster their attempts to gain promotion or to be considered for a new project.

BODYFULNESS

Beyond a verbal message, which is often the main focus in a strategic presentation during a decision-making meeting or a negotiation, Wise Growth has experimented with creating a greater awareness of the *physicality* of a woman leader's approach in her encounters. Exercises and debriefings can help participants to discover their construction and rendering of confidence, assertiveness, and authority (or lack thereof) and who these manifest in their posture and demeanor. These aspects, which are often invisible to a woman, although they are visible or at least implicit to an observant observer, can create a less than desirable impact on the intended audience. Techniques used in theater and improvisation can enable a greater self-awareness of one's movements and gestures and can help one to develop the skills to create behaviors that are coherent with one's target audience.

DEVELOPING VISIBILITY

Although even introverted male candidates can fail to put themselves forward for the next new opportunity, women are particularly guilty of failing to promote themselves. There is very often an assumption that "the good work they are doing is all that is needed" and that it "speaks for itself." Often a little help will make such good work more visible. Women need to let their managers, their sponsors, and the shakers and movers in their organization know that they are interested in the next challenging assignment, that they are ready to advance. They might need to create an alliance with a sponsor or more extroverted colleague who can cite their key contributions and effectively "sell" the qualities of a quieter or more self-effacing contributor.

INFLUENCING AND POWER DYNAMICS

In many cultures, the socialization patterns of boys and girls are such that girls are less accustomed than boys to being in competitive positions, seeking power and "playing the games'" that may accompany such power dynamics. This can often translate into women feeling far less comfortable with this kind of context in corporate life. In some cases, the quest for power may even be seen as somewhat corrupt and unethical and may even suggest the need to "play dirty," which is anathema to many women and men.

A MULTITUDE OF APPROACHES TO INFLUENCING

And yet there are many shades and approaches to wielding influence, and these can be explored and practiced in workshops. Cooperative or *pull* approaches, somewhat more common among women and younger people, are often the most effective approaches for long-term solutions, while less overt than *push* techniques or grand-standing tactics. Staggering your request, knowing when to engage key actors, evaluating the potential support levels you may get for a particular business idea or strategy are key to knowing when and how to make the right moves. Gaining these skills is critical for those wishing to develop their leadership skills and make it up the corporate ladder or to be given the opportunity to lead a team. Gaining legitimacy and credibility are key, and may be undertaken in different ways in different corporate and national cultures; workshop participants can benefit from getting a better understanding of the options open to them in different circumstances.

STRESS MANAGEMENT

- Disproportionate stress; double standards
- Beyond work and family life, no time for myself
- Excellence anxiety afflicts female high achievers

A number of studies have indicated that women tend to perceive higher stress levels associated with top corporate responsibilities. The first stressors are often achieving balance with personal life, since women tend to set a higher standard of what is considered acceptable concerning contact time with children and family than men. If one has been socialized in cultures that emphasize women's responsibility for nurturing, it is difficult to reconcile this with a life spent working 80-hour to 100-hour weeks and collecting frequent flyer miles crisscrossing the globe to attain company objectives. The balancing of priorities is often quite different, and what is important and what matters differ for many female leaders. Here, the Achilles heel is often a feeling of guilt or lack of satisfaction with the balance of how one's time is really engaged at ground level. Missing your child's recital at school or not being in town when they are sick are experiences no mother takes lightly, even if their partner is there to do this.

In a study done by and reported in *Harvard Business Review*, it was found that men compare themselves to the traditional provider, and determine that "10 minutes seeing the kids at night is more important than 10 minutes at work" ("Managing," 2014, p. 62). It is hard to imagine a woman congratulating herself for spending 10 minutes an evening with her kids, but some men consider such behavior "exemplary" ("Managing," 2014).

In the professional-personal life equation, care for others tends to take up almost all the available time on the personal side of things, leaving little or no time for oneself ... time to enjoy one's hobbies, pastimes, sports, exercise, or other activities not dedicated to one's family. Thus, it is difficult to recharge your batteries when you are constantly running on empty. Again, guilt creates a situation in which women will rarely even suggest or ask their families for some "time off for me," and if they do, unless there is enthusiastic encouragement ("Go ahead, Mom, I'm fine!"), many then find it hard to enjoy such time, however brief they may be.

Women also suffer disproportionately from *excellence anxiety*, even when they attain amazing achievements, especially if the results are in the traditionally male bastions of science and technology. They can be made to feel, even at a young age (e.g., in secondary school) as if they have somehow got it all wrong, and that *they will be disliked and unpopular owing to their success*. This can lead to additional stress and fear of exclusion, especially from social activities and partnering options. There is almost an automatic judgment if a woman develops her career to the upper echelons, that she is somehow be less "feminine" or she must have sacrificed her family and personal life, labeled a "hard woman" or "married to the company."

PERFECTIONISM

Often, the flip side of the coin of the tendency to self-criticize and a lack of self-confidence is a zealous perfectionism, a demanding of this of herself and of others in her entourage. Obtaining less than 100% of the desired results can result in self-flagellation and recrimination and internal dialog such as "If only I had done X, the outcome would have been far better." Especially when engaging in an innovative or inherently risky endeavor, it is natural for there to be some degree of failure. When this happens during experimental projects, men tend to attribute failure to the project's risky or uncertain nature, while women tend to attribute it to their lack of ability or of not enough hours worked toward the results. They may repeatedly dwell on negative aspects, replaying the "moment of defeat" in their minds, creating a loud mental reverberation that can become such a strong internal dialog that it becomes difficult to drown out the critical voices. When a woman becomes aware that this is a tendency more typical among women leaders, this awareness alone can do wonders to put things into perspective.

INCREASING CREDIBILITY AND VISIBILITY

Every professional woman needs to think strategically about her vision for her life, both personal and professional, and to determine where they want to go and how they want to get there. Often there is lower awareness about the need to create credibility in one's environment in order to have a greater range of opportunities. This may often involve acquiring a variety of experience, having the right degrees, or also being seen as capable of standing up for the company or the team, even in tough times. Inherent in the equation is the need in most environments to gain visibility.

GAINING VISIBILITY

This involves speaking up, taking opportunities to be the one who delivers the presentation, who represents the company in a negotiation, who speaks on behalf of the team in an interdepartmental meeting to bargain about who gets which scarce resources; in a nutshell: *to be seen and to be heard*. It may also mean increasing the frequency of informal and formal networking encounters. Women, more than men, will often rush off at the end of a meeting to get to the next meeting or to return to their offices to get work done. They are often under more pressure to leave work on time and to tend to family responsibilities. Men will often stay the extra few minutes to engage in informal conversations about what is going on in the company, and to get background information on people, places, and politics—all invaluable input, perhaps implicit and less obvious than the information exchanged in the formal meeting, yet perhaps much more significant to getting the complete picture. It may mean volunteering to be on committees, special projects, high-profile assignments such as a short mission abroad, and to present one's candidacy assertively, underlining one's accomplishments and achievements. It will often mean gaining allies who can mention your name or highlight your accomplishments when you are not present, citing results, facts, figures, and relevant examples, so that this information does not remain in the "hidden or lost data trap," buried in the filing cabinet, or in the files saved on one's computer.

WHAT COMPANIES NEED TO DO

To provide more opportunities and not just lip service to gender equality, organizations need to promote training, coaching, and mentoring opportunities to provide support so as to get women up the leadership pipeline. Strong targets supported from the top and accountability to reach the targets with numbers and serious measurements published annually or announced by top management groups are ways to make otherwise hidden objectives visible. Companywide policies to allow male and female employees to lead more balanced lives such as parental leave, day-care facilities or benefits, family leave, and restraint concerning expecting employees to be "always connected" on evenings and weekends, and always at their managers' beck and call, need to be enacted and practiced by role models at top levels and not just presented as vague ideas or wishful thinking about "the way things should be." HR policies need to create standards about equal pay for equal work, and the HR function needs to check that they are being carried out. Sponsoring programs and having some key women leaders in the organization can help to create role models.

WHAT WOMEN NEED TO DO

Women need to take initiative, rather than stand back and expect someone else to be the vehicle of their promotion. Every person, in their own way, needs to be able to present their talents to the company's key movers and shakers, so that their skills and competences are not unknown factors. Women need to ask for feedback and to pay attention to what needs to be done to hone their abilities and not just their formal capabilities in their field, such as accounting, marketing, or finance, but influencing and leadership skills, and all the soft skills so vital to any manager's career. They need to increase their awareness of any self-limiting behaviors, to develop the ability to be assertive not just in word but in spirit and in body, and most of all, *to knock on doors* rather than passively waiting until someone calls them to offer them the next opportunity.

REFERENCES

Bombelli, C. (2009). *Alice in businessland; On becoming a woman leader.* Author.

Heilman, M., & Okimoto, T. (2007). Why are women penalized for success at male tasks. *Journal of Applied Psychology 92*(1).

McKinsey. (2015a). *Women matter, A CEO's guide to gender equality.*

McKinsey. (2015b). *Women in the workplace*.

Managing your work, managing your life. (2014, March 1). *Harvard Business Review*, p. 62.

Mohr, T. S. (2014, August 25). Why women don't apply for jobs unless they're 100% qualified. *Harvard Business Review*. Retrieved from https://hbr.org/2014/08/why-women-dont-apply-for-jobs-unless-theyre-100-qualified

Pollack, E. (2013, October 3). Why There are still so few women in science. *New York Times Magazine*.

OECD Data. (2013). Indicators for developed countries.

Still a man's world, our glass ceiling index. (2016, March 5). *The Economist*, p. 55.

Wise Growth. (2015). *Motivazione e Diversità: Un contributo alla leadership del futuro* [Motivation and diversity: A contribution to the leadership of the future] (Research report). Sesto San Giovanni, Italy: Wise Growth.

CHAPTER 12

WHY RADICAL INNOVATION NEEDS VISIONARY LEADERSHIP

**Tamara Carleton, William Cockayne,
Andreas Larsson, and Bernhard Küppers**

OBJECTIVE

Solving the fuzzy, wicked problems we face in society today all require radical innovation—big change driven by big ideas that can reshape the world. Radical innovation is complex and often expensive, yet creating change at this level requires more than money and an idea. Driving radical innovation requires leadership with vision. Visionary leadership is leadership that motivates others to share the vision and focuses on the core values at the heart of the vision. Companies can learn much about how to nurture visionary leadership by looking to the long-term success of the U.S. Defense Advanced Research Projects Agency (DARPA), the government agency dedicated to pursuing high-risk and high-reward big ideas. DARPA's approach is top to bottom, from its organizational mandate to its *DARPA Hard* project criteria to its hiring practices, all of which support network flexibility and visionary thinking. Leaders in other contexts—including large companies, small startups, and social enterprises—can integrate lessons from DARPA into their efforts to achieve radical innovation.

Advanced Leadership Insights: How to Lead People and Organizations to Ultimate Success
pp. 143–157
Copyright © 2017 by Information Age Publishing

BIG THINKING LEADS TO BIG CHANGE

Radical innovation is a way of imagining big ideas that can yield significant impact, via a new technology or an approach that creates an entirely new market or that solves a big problem in a new way. The scale and quality of the core idea behind a radical innovation is vastly different from a typical idea for a new product or service. In some cases, the solution pushes the limits of existing technology; in fact, building the solution may require the creation of new technologies.

Netflix is a great example of thinking big. Launched in 1998, Netflix aimed to change the movie rentals business, initially by providing viewers with convenient mail-in DVD subscriptions and then by reshaping the entire business of television by offering users instant streaming of video content. While Netflix did not change the technical infrastructure of the post office or the Internet, it developed multiple data algorithms that deeply changed how people engage with entertainment. These algorithms categorized the spectrum of shows and then connected user behaviors to these categories, ultimately creating a new taxonomy of subgenres that automatically adjusted to user preferences. Chris Jaffe, vice president of user interface innovation at Netflix, told Engadget, "[We have] 75 million members around the world; essentially that means 75 million different experiences" (Alvarez, 2016, para. 4). Netflix is challenging and altering how television and movies are produced and delivered by funding original shows around concepts developed based on the company's vast pool of user data and betting on new compression algorithms that deliver highly dynamic range programming.

Why do these big ideas matter? At a practical level, the problems faced by society and organizations are more wicked and fuzzy than ever, so merely cutting costs and lead times while gradually improving quality is no longer sufficient to address these problems. Neither industry nor society can continue to go through the same motions when both industry partners and users demand drastic change. At an emotional level, energetic engagement with a big idea, even one that seems impossibly out of reach, can feed big change. In the 1960s, for instance, the United States committed to sending a person to the moon. Technologically, the goal was audaciously optimistic, yet the U.S. government committed the required resources, and in 1969, Neil Armstrong became the first person to walk on the moon. The effort not only achieved a huge scientific milestone, it also delivered countless technological innovations and economic growth to society as a whole.

Or consider Japan in the 1980s, when the country's Ministry of International Trade and Industry had the big idea to advance the state of computer processing. In pursuit of this idea, the ministry organized a national R&D program to create technologies that would leapfrog other countries' capabilities. Called *fifth-generation computing*, the idea inspired similar programs around the world. United States policymakers responded by creating a series of *grand challenges* to fund new computing solutions. Ultimately, Japan's vision advanced knowledge worldwide about high-performance and parallel computing, which in turn influenced the global information technology industry in the following decades.

Driving these kinds of big ideas—developing them from inspiration to execution and pushing them out into the world—requires strong leadership. Such leadership can emerge in many contexts. In large corporations, visionary leaders drive breakthrough commercial innovations that reach new markets or change entire product categories; in government agencies or university programs, they foster large-scale innovation to support broad, overarching goals; as entrepreneurs, they build startup companies that bring new technologies to market, sometimes reshaping the market in the process. And as part of social enterprises, these leaders harness entrepreneurial energies to solve social problems at both micro- and macrolevels. All these levels represent radical innovation driven by big ideas—and shaped by the vision of strong leadership teams.

THE POWER OF BIG IDEAS

Thus, radical innovation is big change driven by big ideas, since the creation of new and very different solutions in the form of new technologies, products, or services, or new frameworks or business models. Radical innovation is fundamentally different from incremental innovation—the types of small adjustments and upgrades we are used to seeing regularly in products, which is driven by analysis (O'Connor, Leifer, Paulson, & Peters, 2008). While incremental innovation relies on market research and *customer voices* tools, radical innovation relies on experimentation. Learning takes place by doing, often through deliberate prototyping and iteration. While incremental innovation seeks answers, an agenda of radical innovation is typically driven by questions, because questions reveal possible directions for new thinking and growth. Asking a question starts dialogue and triggers reflection. Seeking answers too quickly can limit the consideration of other options and can overly narrow the field of exploration. Steve Jobs, who led the tech company Apple through its most innovative period, famously eschewed market research and relied instead on his intuition, which led him to radical products like the Mac computer, iPod, iPhone, and iPad. Jobs once said, "You can't just ask customers what they want and then try to give that to them. By the time you get it built, they'll want something new" (Burlingham, 1989, para. 8).

Radical innovation is sometimes conflated with *big R&D*, which is about large-scale programs, typically government-led, that address an overarching technical challenge, often connected to a large social problem. In U.S. history, these projects tend to emerge from political pressures to address external threats or social needs. Thomas Hughes (2000) has documented several such projects in U.S history. For instance, the Semi-Automatic Ground Environment air-defense project, initiated in the 1950s, proposed an automated control system for tracking and intercepting enemy bomber aircraft in real time. Given that capabilities in interactive computing and data communications were only just emerging at the time, this vision was very bold indeed. Achieving it required more than 800 programmers and the technical resources of some of the largest U.S. corporations, such as IBM.

These large programs have many moving parts and numerous stakeholders. Unlike many corporate radical innovation endeavors, or even ambitious startups, these programs do not aspire to create monumental change from a single organization or effort. Rather, the goal is to accomplish a bigger end by distributing action across multiple parties. Like radical innovation, *big R&D* may be focused on exponential impact, but this impact is achieved in increments, as each player contributes. Rather than the big effort demanded by radical innovation at the organizational level, *big R&D* relies on cumulative effort across organizations. Indeed, the individual contributions may themselves be radical innovations, driven by particular visions around the solution to a particular piece of the problem, or focused on a particular technical domain.

Regardless, radical innovation and *big R&D* share one key characteristic: the big idea at the center of an effort. Big ideas imagine a solution orders of magnitude bigger or better than what exists. Big ideas are audacious; they are intended to change existing paradigms. Their success cannot be gauged using the usual metrics of incremental innovation; the potential rewards are enormous—at least as great as the risk involved. Above all, these ideas are driven by a vision, a compelling picture of the future that draws broader support from others and propels the work to achieve this vision.

COMMON MECHANISMS FOR RADICAL INNOVATION

Clearly, making a big idea work—bringing a radical innovation to market—can pay off very well in terms of financial performance and societal benefit. Unsurprisingly, companies and researchers have tried to define the exact formula for bringing a radical innovation to fruition. However, in spite of all these efforts, the precise recipe for achieving radical innovation remains unclear.

Large corporations have been particularly eager to find a process for producing radical innovation on demand. Managers have experimented with a number of mechanisms, most commonly a combination of intrapreneurial, skunkworks-type organizations, and corporate venturing units (O'Connor et al., 2008). Intrapreneuring relies on enterprising individual employees to provide big ideas and the leadership to develop them. Intrapreneurs act as entrepreneurs-in-residence, taking direct responsibility for turning their ideas into profitable businesses within the framework of the corporation. In the skunkworks approach, originally developed by Lockheed Martin (Johnson & Smith 1989), companies make use of a small group of experts, protecting them from the company's regular bureaucratic processes and financial performance metrics, so they can work on a risky project through unconventional means. Well-known examples of products developed through a skunkworks-type organization include Lockheed Martin's XP-80 jet fighter and Apple's original Macintosh computer (Levy, 2000). Corporate venturing units invest strategically in startups that are developing promising new technologies that the sponsoring company hopes to acquire or adopt, once their viability and marketability has been proven. Unfortunately, none of these approaches have offered reliable results.

However, one approach suggests where at least part of the answer may lie. Corporate venturing units emerged in recognition of the fact that startups tend to succeed more often at radical innovation than established companies. These small, agile organizations are seen as more capable of gauging market needs and respond to emerging ideas. Also, entrepreneurs tend to establish companies around a vision—a big idea that seeks to develop a new technology, access a new market, or solve a problem. Successful entrepreneurs come from a wide range of backgrounds and have highly varied skills sets. What they share is the ability to convince others—cofounders, investors, potential employees—of the power of their vision. But, like corporate attempts at radical innovation, startups fail more often than they succeed, sometimes for pragmatic reasons: a technology fails, or regulatory obstacles cannot be overcome. Yet the first sign of a failing startup is often a loss of faith in the vision on the part of those supporting the company—investors withdraw funding or will not offer more, key employees leave, or customers don't buy in.

Indeed, scholars generally argue that the failure of radical innovation in established companies can be traced to a lack of the right kind of leadership. Studies show that the effective pursuit of radical innovation effectively requires different leadership, different skills sets, and even a different organizational culture than incremental innovation. As innovation scholar Rob Dekkers (2005) points out, "Where incremental innovation reinforces the capabilities of established organizations, radical innovation does force them to ask a new set of questions, to draw on new technical and commercial skills, and to employ new problem-solving approaches" (pp. 189–190). Resisting the natural tendency to default to familiar practices, such as judging radical and incremental innovation ideas by the same criteria, requires a leader who shares the vision captured by the big idea at the heart of the project.

VISION IN SMALL AND MEDIUM-SIZED ENTERPRISES

Organizations of all sizes benefit from having a vision to drive their actions. Founding teams at small and medium-sized enterprises must also seek to enlist others to help them build and deliver a radical innovation's vision. Small and medium-sized enterprise leaders know they must access different skills sets and know-how, as well as the means and infrastructure, to turn a raw concept into a scalable and successful business. Convincing others to join the effort requires a vision strong enough to overcome the doubts and risks of employees, partners, and especially investors. However, compelling as the market analysis or prototype may be, supporters of an early venture ultimately enlist out of faith—an inherent belief in the vision of a founding team. That team must be able to build a chain of enthusiasm for the company's promise of exponential impact. Knowing how to reach people's hearts, how to motivate employees through all stages of growth, means understanding the basic psychology of how people work (Bösenberg & Küppers, 2011). While this understanding holds true for people in any setting, big or small, it is particularly relevant to startup cultures, where faith in the driving vision may be the only personal reward for an extended time.

A current example is Hyperloop Technologies, a U.S. startup with a vision of supersonic transportation. Dubbed the "fifth mode of transport" by the team—following the four dominant modes of land, air, sea, and space—the Hyperloop solution would move people and cargo through reduced-pressure tubes by using linear induction motors and air-compressors. In 2012, billionaire inventor Elon Musk, the founder of Tesla Motors and SpaceX, became frustrated with the bullet train system under proposal in California, and ultimately outlined an idea for two massive tubes between San Francisco and Los Angeles that would ferry pressurized pods moving at up to 700 miles per hour (1,127 km/h). A trip that normally takes 6 hours by car between these two cities could theoretically take 35 minutes. The Hyperloop team is looking to launch a working solution by 2020. Shervin Pishevar, cofounder and chairman of Hyperloop Technologies, told a reporter that "Moonshot ideas can happen faster than any other time in history.... It took really courageous investors, including Elon, to put up a lot capital just to prove a rocket could get into space. The same is true for Hyperloop. There are courageous investors who believe in this and want to see it exist" (Lipton, 2016, para. 4).

Needless to say, big visions are not limited to startups in California. Vision is a key driver in the success of what the German business author Hermann Simon (1996) has dubbed *hidden champions*—largely unknown, mid-sized companies that are world leaders in their markets. According to Simon, these companies tend to be goal-oriented, driven by the vision to be number one in their industry. Their employees tend to express high loyalty and identification with the company and its vision. Unsurprisingly, these companies are mostly led by their founders. In other words, the founder's vision continues to shape the company and its success.

One example of a hidden champion is Baader (2016), a German food processing machinery manufacturer. As its corporate philosophy makes clear, the company focuses on "total solutions with quality in all phases." As one of the "strongest and most innovative" business partners in global food processing, Baader seeks to develop state-of-the-art equipment to make food processing safer, more efficient, and more profitable. In its internal and external communication, Baader focuses on innovation and high quality, based on the core principle that "value follows innovation". This commitment is reflected in the company's actions: It invests 12% of its annual revenues in innovation; 75 of its 450 employees (nearly 17%) at headquarters are in R&D. Every engineer or developing leader at Baader must work in R&D at some point in order to move forward, ensuring close engagement with the R&D function among both engineers and general management. This commitment delivers results—the company files an average of 44 new patents every year—one patent for every two R&D employees every year.

To accomplish its goals, Baader maintains control of its entire value chain. Its innovative leadership is strengthened by clearly defined roles and the flexibility to allow for adjustments by the engineers at every stage of design and production. The company's decision-making process is very comprehensive and effective (Joseph, 2013). The family-owned company's leaders are closely involved, and personnel decisions are made very carefully; the company's relationships with all its employees is based on trust. As a result, the company routinely attracts the best food engineers from German universities, assuring a steady flow of the talent it needs to support its innovation agenda.

VISION IN SOCIAL ENTERPRISES

Vision is an exceptionally strong driver in social businesses. A social business, as defined by the Nobel Peace Prize winner Muhammad Yunus (2007), is a cause-driven enterprise. It is not a charity or a pure welfare activity; rather, a social business seeks to compensate its owners and workers while optimizing products and services for markets that commercial businesses don't usually serve. A social business can make money—enough to cover the cost of salaries, R&D, marketing, and so on—by producing a product that its target consumers can afford. The value proposition here often represents a radical innovation, since the combination of new products or services and new users leads to the creation of an entirely new market, resulting in what IDEO design consultants Ryan Jacoby and Diego Rodriguez (2007) consider to be *revolutionary* growth.

Visionary leadership is crucial to social enterprises, because they act in contexts where traditional notions of markets and consumers do not entirely apply. Those who will ultimately benefit most from the products or services offered by these companies often lack both money and education—in other words, potential consumers might lack both awareness of why a product or service might be valuable to them and the funds to pay for the products. As a result, these markets are not fully functional by conventional definitions, and social enterprises have difficulty developing long-term strategies that allow them to scale successfully. Thus, a social enterprise's ability to create and grow its market strongly depends on the team's ability to envision a new workable future and, most importantly, to compel other groups to join it in realizing this vision.

In spite of obstacles, some social enterprises do succeed. For instance, Proximity Designs, an award-winning social enterprise based in Myanmar (formerly Burma), has been successful in developing the country's smallholder agricultural sector (Osberg & Martin, 2015). Proximity Designs understood that rural farmers needed pumps and irrigation products that were effective, durable, and affordable, yet these farmers could not acquire these products through established channels because they lacked access to governmental support. Existing businesses overlooked rural famers as a potential customer base because larger and more sophisticated farmers could more readily afford advanced equipment. Proximity filled the gap by combining low-cost product design and development with a suite of services tailored to rural farmers, including microcredit product financing, crop loans, and farm advisory services.

Another social business, Ped-World, has developed a way to use fog collectors to gather water from low clouds. Gathering water in this way requires no large or complex machines; the fog collectors are large, yet easy to assemble. Volunteer engineers work with local townspeople in Africa (e.g., Tanzania) to put together the machines; they share a vision to deliver water solutions to places where water is unsafe or inaccessible. Founded in 2006 and operating from Germany, Ped-World today is still controlled by its founders, and most of its core team abroad has remained the same from the early years. Critically, this core team maintains the company's focus on innovation, and this long-term engagement means personnel in the various countries and at headquarters identify strongly with a project.

Traditional companies may also engage in social enterprises, besides to their usual business. For instance, when Yunus (2007) sought a way to address the problem of hookworm, he approached the multinational sportswear company Adidas for help. Hookworm, a parasite that enters the body through the soles of the feet, is common in Africa because poor people tend to walk around without shoes. Eliminating hookworm is simple—if people wear shoes, parasites cannot enter the body. The obstacle was that any shoe had to be perceived as affordable and attractive for the target population to adopt it; otherwise, people would prefer to go barefoot, as usual. Yunus convinced Adidas to develop a USD$1 shoe, and Adidas embraced the challenge. In many ways, beginning with the product price, this is a radical approach to the innovation process because the price goal drives all the product planning, design, and manufacturing. In assembling a project team, Adidas approached only high-potential employees—those known for their ability to find inventive solutions. These creators were energized by Yunus's vision—the idea of finding an affordable solution to a significant health problem, which in turn would strategically give Adidas a presence in a new market.

VISIONARY LEADERSHIP AT DARPA

The kind of forward-looking leadership that drives radical innovation—across large corporations, small hidden champions, and social enterprises—is marked by a commitment to building a bold vision and making it real. One U.S. government agency has exemplified visionary leadership since its inception, producing breakthrough after breakthrough for more than 50 years. A look at DARPA's culture and processes shows how visionary leadership can be cultivated in an organization to produce radical innovation on a regular basis.

Founded in 1958 by the U.S. government, the Defense Advanced Research Projects Agency (DARPA), pursues big ideas—those its managers judge to be *DARPA Hard*, the agency's term for very ambitious technical challenges that seem almost impossible to achieve (Carleton, 2010). DARPA has built an incredible track record of developing world-changing innovations. Well-known examples include ARPANET, which became the foundation for the Internet; the global positioning satellite (GPS) system; speech recognition technology; and aircraft stealth technology (Belfiore, 2009). Although some of these inventions may eventually have emerged in their own time, DARPA's support accelerated their invention and development. Further, by releasing the commercial applications of these inventions to companies and the public domain, DARPA amplified their impacts on a grander scale. And while nearly all of DARPA's big ideas originated in the United States—and all were developed by the agency to serve U.S. purposes—they all ultimately reshaped industries, and lives, worldwide.

What is the secret to DARPA's success? There are numerous reasons why the agency functions exceptionally well as an organization of big ideas; it operates under a model that demands and supports visionary leadership at every level (Bonvillian, 2006). This model has only three essential elements: a clear mandate, an open network structure, and simple hiring criteria that highlight visionary leadership at least as much as technical expertise (Carleton, 2010).

First, the agency has a clear mandate for radical innovation. At an organizational level, DARPA's mission is to maintain the technological superiority of the U.S. military—and to prevent technological surprises from harming U.S. national security—by sponsoring revolutionary, high-payoff research that bridges the gap between fundamental discoveries and their military uses (DARPA, 2009). Since the agency was founded, this mandate has provided steadfast direction to internal members and external constituents. Under this mandate, typically six DARPA office directors operate their own portfolio of big ideas, grouped around a general theme such as *microsystems* or *biological technologies*. While government-led, DARPA projects are not large-scale efforts that involve hundreds of people, as is usually the case in *big R&D*; instead, its projects are smaller and highly concentrated efforts, each focused on a separate big idea.

Second, the agency is structured to support radical innovation through a wide network of contributors and collaborators. DARPA does not maintain any research facilities or labs of its own; most of the work occurs off-site at the organizations it funds. These include companies, universities, national laboratories, nonprofit research organizations, federally funded R&D centers, and U.S. military services. Together, these organizations function as a powerful distributed network, with DARPA providing two key drivers: vision and funding (Figure 12.1). This network model brings two key benefits. First, it maximizes the diversity of inputs, since new ideas may come from any source in the network, allowing another layer of leadership to emerge. Second, the network maximizes the impacts of the ideas under development, because a new idea diffuses across multiple organizations throughout the network.

Third, and perhaps most importantly, DARPA's hiring practices guarantee a dynamic organizational culture and provide explicit support for visionary leadership. Program managers may be recruited from anywhere in the agency's network; they work at DARPA for only typically 3 to 4

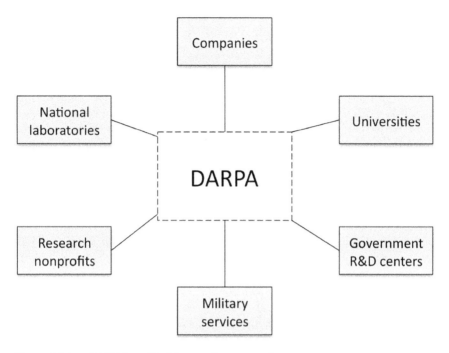

Figure 12.1.   DARPA's radical innovation network.

years. This policy keeps the organizational culture dynamic by regularly infusing new ideas and visions through short cycles of intense innovation. Thus, new directors and program managers must be able to think big in a compressed time frame. Further, they are hired as technical visionaries – they are expected to start the job with a vision, essentially a big idea that requires large-scale technological innovation, something truly *DARPA Hard*. They are solely responsible for shaping, spearheading, and promoting their visions throughout their DARPA tenure. As a result, as science writer David Malakoff (1999, p. 66) notes, "some [program managers] become influential figures in their subfields, capable of nudging established research communities in a particular direction or creating collaborations where none existed before."

This focus on vision is supported by a flexible structure that allows DARPA program managers to freely pursue their visions. Aside from legally required contractual procedures and standard reporting, DARPA does not enforce many processes in its organization. The agency's leadership trusts program managers to create and develop their visions with little guidance. From the day they are hired, DARPA program managers drive the vision-setting for their individual initiatives. When a program manager feels his or her vision is clear, they will pitch the vision as a new program and will secure funding from the agency director. While the technological idea at the core of the vision drives action, the path to the vision is emergent, driven by recursive exploration and direct engagement with researchers in the field. Program managers may spend up to 18 months getting their visions right before proceeding to a formal program launch and project solicitation. During that time, they are constantly out in the field, interacting with teams and potential members of the network, scouting for new ideas, and comparing observations with their big visions. In developing their visions, program managers typically turn to two processes for support and learning: expert workshops and proofs-of-concept (Figure 12.2).

Expert workshops are invitation-only, small group discussions between a DARPA program manager and select members of an R&D community, typically taking place away from DARPA offices over 2 to 3 days. These discussions, which primarily involve experts in a particular problem domain, emphasize the exchange of ideas and the demonstration and application of a potential new technology. The objective is to gather feedback about a topic, its potential technical issues, and an overall direction for development. These workshops are effective because they draw on collective wisdom in a field, giving program managers access to the latest knowledge about a particular topic.

If workshops rely on people, then proofs-of-concept focus on ideas. A proof-of-concept explores and tests the feasibility of an emerging idea through a directed demonstration of its potential execution. Proofs-of-concept are a form of prototyping. They may be presented as written documentation, physical artifacts, or software simulations that confirm initial assumptions. Generally, in seeking a proof-of-concept, a DARPA program manager will provide a set of early requirements to an R&D entity, which

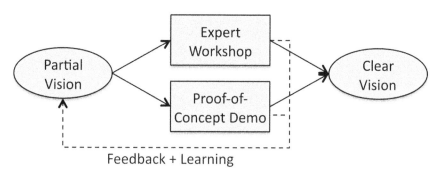

Figure 12.2.   DARPA's process of formulating technology visions for radical innovation,

then undertakes the project as a paid assignment. By working closely with a network partner, a program manager can test early hunches before undertaking a new technical initiative.

At DARPA, the process of developing a vision is recursive and iterative. Ideally, a feedback and learning loop occurs at every iteration. For both expert workshops and proofs-of-concept, the objective is to gain continual learning and feedback from the relevant R&D community, which then is used to sharpen the original big idea.

While most enterprises lack DARPA's funding—almost U.S.$2.9 billion for FY2016 (DARPA, 2016)—leaders in almost any organization type can adapt many of the elements of the agency's approach to their own innovation efforts. For instance: Encourage your R&D groups to think big and insist that they craft mandates, which will give explicit permission for them to be audacious and seek opportunities. Challenge your project managers to find their own baseline for new ideas, similar to DARPA's *DARPA Hard* concept, that pushes their ideas to visionary potential. Deliberately hire for vision, so that it is a requirement in job postings and new employee interviews. Reward senior executives who develop the next generation of leaders who can drive their visions of change, especially when these visions are partially ready and *half-baked*. And experiment often, integrating the two DARPA mechanisms of expert workshops and proofs-of-concept into the early stages of idea testing.

CONCLUSION

Big ideas are crucial to driving progress for humanity. But whether these ideas emerge from a large, established company looking to create a new market, a startup seeking to gain a foothold, or a social enterprise working to solve some of the most basic problems of poverty, realizing a big idea is extraordinarily difficult. The challenge is exemplified by the dismal success rate of corporate attempts at radical innovation, as well as by the very high failure rate even for startups with truly new technology to offer.

The key ingredient required bring a big idea into the world is visionary leadership. Incremental innovation—small improvements and predictable changes—can be developed from concrete, data-based models, from thinking that focuses on answering defined questions. But radical innovation—the practice of implementing big ideas—reaches beyond known, or even knowable, answers. Radical innovation requires a focus on questions rather than answers, on imagination rather than data, and—ultimately—on vision. These differences mean that leaders who would drive radical innovation must have different skills. The most important of these skills is the ability to clearly express a vision and to convince others to share it, not just at the outset but throughout the long, hard process of bringing it to fruition.

The future belongs to big ideas. Smart organizations, whether seeking market success or new approaches to solving the world's most wicked problems, will look for ways to identify and support their visionary leaders.

ACKNOWLEDGMENT

The authors are grateful to MaryAnne Gobble for her thoughtful review and edits to this chapter.

REFERENCES

Alvarez, E. (2016). Netflix is going all in on HDR and more original content. *Engadget webzine*. Retrieved from http://www.engadget.com/2016/02/23/netflix-hdr-original-content-mwc-2016/

Baader. (2016). *Philosophy*. Retrieved from https://www.baader.com/en/baader_group/philosophy/index.html

Belfiore, M. (2009). *The department of mad scientists: How DARPA is remaking our world, from the Internet to artificial limbs*. New York, NY: Smithsonian Books/HarperCollins.

Bercovici, J. (2015). Slack is our company of the year: Here's why everybody's talking about it. *Inc.* Retrieved from http://www.inc.com/magazine/201512/jeff-bercovici/slack-company-of-the-year-2015.html

Bösenberg, C., & Küppers, B. (2011). *Im mittelpunkt steht der mitarbeiter* [The employees are your most valuable asset]. München, Germany: Haufe-Verlag.

Burlingham, B. (1989). The entrepreneur of the decade: An interview with Steven Jobs, Inc.'s entrepreneur of the decade. *Inc.* Retrieved from http://www.inc.com/magazine/19890401/5602.html

Carleton, T. L. (2010). *The value of vision in radical technological innovation* (PhD dissertation). School of Engineering, Stanford University, CA.

Defense Advanced Research Projects Agency. (2009). *Strategic plan*. Washington, DC: Author.

Defense Advanced Research Projects Agency. (2016). *Budget*. Retrieved from http://www.darpa.mil/about-us/budget

Dekkers, R. (2005). *(R)evolution: Organizations and the dynamics of the environment*. New York, NY: Springer Science+Business Media.

Hughes, T. P. (2000). *Rescuing Prometheus: Four monumental projects that changed the modern world*. New York, NY: Vintage.

Jacoby, R., & Rodriguez, D. (2007). *Innovation, growth, and getting to where you want to go. Design Management Review, 18*(1), 10–15.

Johnson, C. L., & Smith, M. (1989). *Kelly: More than my share of it all*. Washington, DC: Smithsonian.

Joseph, U. A. (2013). *The "Made in Germany" champion brands: Nation branding, innovation and world export leadership*. New York, NY: Routledge.

Levy, S. (2000). *Insanely great: The life and times of Macintosh, the computer that changed everything*. New York, NY: Penguin Books.

Lipton, J. (2016). Hyperloop will be here in 2020 and the impact will be huge. *CNBC.com*. Retrieved from http://www.cnbc.com/2016/03/07/hyperloop-will-be-here-in-2020-and-the-impact-will-be-huge.html

Malakoff, D. (1999). Pentagon agency thrives on in-your-face science. *Science, 285*(5433), 1476–1480.

O'Connor, G. C., Leifer, R., Paulson, A., & Peters, L. (2008). *Grabbing lightning: Building a capability for breakthrough innovation*. San Francisco, CA: Jossey-Bass.

Osberg, S. R., & Martin, R. (2015). Two keys to sustainable social enterprise. *Harvard Business Review, 93*(5), 86–94.

Simon, H. (1996). *Hidden champions: Lessons from 500 of the world's best unknown companies*. Boston, MA: Harvard Business School Press.

Yunus, M. (2007). *Creating a world without poverty: Social business and the future of capitalism*. New York, NY: Public Affairs.

CHAPTER 13

LEADERS AS MASTERS OF CHANGE

Marios I. Katsioloudes and Vicky Katsioloudes

OBJECTIVE

When businesspeople are asked what effective leaders do, one gets answers such as: they set strategy; they motivate; they create culture; they have a vision; they create a mission; they lead people, and so on. One rarely hears an answer such as, they bring change to an organization. Leaders and change are not separate entities. They should be looked at as interrelated. Leaders should be agents and masters of change.

LEADERS AS MASTER OF CHANGE

The notion of leaders as masters of change is pertinent to today's business reality, in which globalization and rapid technological advancements increase the pressure on organizations to be innovative and to be responsive to the external environment, accelerating the pace of organizational change. So, if change seems to be the only constant in organizational reality, how do we ensure that leaders are effective masters of change? We present three insights, based on decades of work with leaders.

Advanced Leadership Insights: How to Lead People and Organizations to Ultimate Success
pp. 159–164
Copyright © 2017 by Information Age Publishing

Insight 1: Leaders as Learners

First, leaders must be learners. To be a change master means that you must first be able to change yourself (Moran, Harris, & Moran, 2011).

Successful leadership styles are dependent to a degree on the people and their cultures at a given point in time (Moran et al., 2011). A leader should "empower people, so that they will, in turn, develop their own as well as the organization's potential … to meet that challenge leaders should be planned change makers, beginning with one's self" (p. 124).

As already mentioned in previous chapters of this book, Goleman (2000) introduced six leadership styles usually used by executives. These styles are not exclusive or used in a vacuum, but should be used in combination, according to the situation at hand and the profiles of the organization's employees.

Coercive style: In this style, a leader acts as a "dictator"—he or she imposes on employees the way and the means to achieve the organizational goals, which are set by the leader.

Authoritative style: While the leader provides the future direction and sets goals for employees to achieve, they are free to choose the ways to achieve these goals.

Affiliative style: The leader's priority here is people and of course they come first. This leadership style is ideal for building team spirit and increase morale.

Democratic style: The leader encourages the employees to have a voice in decision-making and as a result a flexible and responsible organization is being established where fresh ideas are eventually generated.

Pace-setting style: The leader sets high standards for performance for the employees, and he/she demonstrates high performance, that in turn has a positive impact on self-motivated and competent employees.

Coaching style: The leader masters the change in his or her employees' personal development. When employees are aware of their weaknesses and desire change, the leader can contribute to changing employees' ways.

Boaz and Fox (2014) emphasize that one cannot separate organizational change from individual change. It is important for leaders to identify their strengths and limitations, to recognize their motivations and drives, and to be aware of the leadership styles they employ. This requires that they question core assumptions about themselves and the way things work and that they take what Joseph Campbell calls the *hero's journey*—stepping outside one's comfort zone so as to experience trials and adventures.

Insight 2: Leaders Must Actively Work to Close the Skills Gaps for Effective Change Agents

Rosabeth Moss Kanter (2005) identified seven fundamental skills used by leaders of successful change efforts (also see Figure 13.1):

1. **Tuning in to the environment**: Actively collect information to gain knowledge about what is going on inside and outside your organization, and pay attention to broad signs of change (e.g., competitors doing something differently).

2. **Kaleidoscope thinking**: Challenge the prevailing organizational wisdom and question long-standing assumptions; look through a different lens to find different solutions to a problem; and create circumstances that promote kaleidoscopic thinking (e.g., large brainstorming sessions, interdisciplinary teams).

3. **Communicating a compelling vision**: Make a compelling case for the change you are pursuing; communicate an aspiration, not just a picture of what could be; and appeal to the need to better ourselves and participate in helping to build the company's future.

4. **Getting buy-in and building coalitions**: Find key supporters and influencers into, across, and outside the organization who will champion your ideas; and gain valuable feedback in the process.

<table>
<tr><td colspan="2" align="center">**The 7 Skills of Change Masters**</td></tr>
<tr><td>Skill #1</td><td>Tuning in to the environment</td></tr>
<tr><td>Skill #2</td><td>Kaleidoscope thinking</td></tr>
<tr><td>Skill #3</td><td>Communicating a compelling vision</td></tr>
<tr><td>Skill #4</td><td>Getting buy-in, Building coalitions</td></tr>
<tr><td>Skill #5</td><td>Nurturing the working team</td></tr>
<tr><td>Skill #6</td><td>Persisting and perservering</td></tr>
<tr><td>Skill #7</td><td>Making everyone a hero</td></tr>
</table>

Figure 13.1.   Based on the HBR article *Leadership for Change: Enduring Skills for Change Masters*, by Rosabeth Moss Kanter (November, 2005).

5. **Nurturing the working team**: Form a working team that will focus on implementing the change initiatives, and support these initiatives; and develop a broad outline and allow the team to explore new possibilities.

6. **Persisting and persevering**: Leaders must persist and persevere, particularly in the midst of change, when hard work is needed to make change efforts sustainable.

7. **Making everyone a hero**: Recognize, celebrate, and reward the people involved in the change process; this not only brings the change cycle to its logical conclusion, it also keeps people motivated to attempt change again.

Leadership development programs are a worthwhile option for leaders to acquire the necessary skills and competencies needed to be an effective master of change. A study employing computer simulation techniques indicated that high-quality leadership development interventions yield high monetary returns on leadership development investment (RODI) for upper-level, mid-level, and lower-level leaders (Richards, Holton, & Katsioloudes, 2014). It is important to note, as Senge (1999) reminds us, that masters of change can be found at different levels in the organization —change is not driven solely by a hero-like leader at the top. Instead, there are three leadership levels that drive and support change: (1) imaginative, committed local line leaders, (2) enthusiastic mid-level community builders or network leaders, and (3) executive leaders who, in addition to their accountability for organizational performance, must create an environment of innovation and knowledge generation.

In an interview (Kurma, 2007), the managing director of Tata Motors emphasized the importance of involving leaders at different levels of the organization as masters of change. He said: "If we had tried to go only through the top, we might not have succeeded as well, and the transformation might have taken much longer ... as a means of accelerating change, we identified individuals who would serve as examples to others" (p. 55).

Insight 3: Consider the *Softer* Skills

When asked to define the ideal leader, many people would underline attributes, for instance, knowledge, sturdiness, determination, and vision —qualities generally connected with leadership. Gentler, more individual qualities are often omitted, yet they are crucial. An article on change leaders (De Smet, Lavoie, & Schwartz Hioe, 2012) noted that senior executives often overlook the *softer* skills their leaders will need to make lasting changes throughout the organization. These skills include the ability to inspire managers and workers when they feel overwhelmed, to promote collaboration across organizational boundaries, or to help managers embrace change programs through dialogue rather than dictation (De Smet et al., 2012).

In examining these *softer* skills, one should note that, in the past 20-odd years, researchers have begun to examine emotional intelligence as a predictor of effective leadership. Even though a specific level of diagnostic and specialized expertise is a base necessity for achievement, some studies show that emotional intelligence might be the key quality that recognizes extraordinary performers from the individuals who are simply sufficient. Psychologist and author Daniel Goleman first introduced the phrase *emotional intelligence* in his 1995 book, and connected the idea to business. In his research into almost 200 large, worldwide organizations, Goleman found that viable pioneers have high emotional intelligence (Goleman, 2007). Without it, a person can have top training, a sharp personality, and an interminable supply of smart thoughts, yet he or she may not be a great leader. The main segments of emotional intelligence—mindfulness, self-control, inspiration, empathy, and social aptitude—can sound unbusinesslike. However Goleman, who is cochair of the Consortium for Research on Emotional Intelligence in Organizations at Rutgers University, discovered direct links between emotional intelligence and measurable business results.

CONCLUSION

In a business climate in which globalization and technology are the primary forces of complex change, change seems to be the new norm in organizational reality. Thus, it is imperative, now more than ever, to view leaders and change as interrelated. Organizations should build leaders' change capabilities across organizational levels. The focus on leaders as masters of change should be reflected in executive leadership development programs and business leadership courses.

REFERENCES

Boaz, N., & Fox, E. A. (2014). Change leader, change thyself. *McKinsey Quarterly*. Retrieved from http://www.mckinsey.com/global-themes/leadership/change-leader-change-thyself

De Smet, A., Lavoie, J., & Schwartz Hioe, E. (2012). Developing better change leaders. *McKinsey Quarterly*. Retrieved from http://www.mckinsey.com/business-functions/organization/our-insights/developing-better-change-leaders

Goleman, D. (1995). *Emotional intelligence*. New York, NY: Bantam Book.

Goleman, D. (2000). Leadership that gets results. *Harvard Business Review*. Retrieved from https://hbr.org/2000/03/leadership-that-gets-results

Goleman, D. (2004). What makes a leader. *Harvard Business Review*. Retrieved from https://hbr.org/2004/01/what-makes-a-leader

Kumra, G. (2007). Leading change: An interview with the managing director of Tata Motors. *McKinsey Quarterly*. Retrieved from http://www.mckinsey.com/business-functions/organization/our-insights/leading-change-an-interview-with-the-managing-director-of-tata-motors

Moran, R. T., Harris, P. R., & Moran, S. V. (2011). *Managing cultural differences* (8th ed.). Oxford, England: Elsevier.

Moss Kanter, R. (2005, November 17). *Leadership for change: Enduring skills for change masters*. Harvard Business School Note No. 9-304-062, rev. Boston, MA: HBS Publishing.

Richards, B. W., Holton, E. F., & Katsioloudes, V. (2014). The use of discrete computer simulation modeling to estimate return on leadership development investment. *The Leadership Quarterly, 25*(5), 1054–1068.

Senge, P. M. (1999). *The dance of change: The challenges of sustaining momentum in learning organizations*. New York, NY: Currency/Doubleday.

CHAPTER 14

HOW TO SUCCEED IN A POLITICAL ORGANIZATION

Tobias Mahr and Bertolt Stein

OBJECTIVE

In this chapter we explore how value-driven leaders (people who feel firmly bound to certain standards in attitudes and behaviors such as loyalty, honesty, openness, respect, fairness, justice, integrity, coexistence, and many more) can be successful in a highly political organization.

DO THE VALUE-DRIVEN PEOPLE ALWAYS "LOOSE"?

You have seen it before. When bad things happen in the workplace, rumors start, discussions follow, and groups of different stakeholders form. Eventually, a dispute develops and escalates through various stages. The people involved can be categorized in terms of interest-driven versus value-driven, fair versus unfair, egotistic versus altruistic, and a dozen or more dichotomies. The manifestation of individual behaviors can lead to what people describe as an organization's *political culture*.

We focus on some of these dichotomies: the *good* versus the *bad* and the clever versus the not-so-clever. We seek to influence the dichotomy winners versus the losers. Reflecting on our experiences in the workplace

Advanced Leadership Insights: How to Lead People and Organizations to Ultimate Success
pp. 165–177

related to people we consider value-driven—a term we will discuss—and talked about how they behave and act in situations involving conflicts, clashes, or fights, how they succeed in larger organizations concerning politics or shaping the culture. We asked whether we had ever seen the *good (value-driven people as explained in the following paragraph)* succeed in a clash with the *bad (not value-driven people)*. Sadly, the answer was *no*. Not once!

Here, we discuss possible reasons for these frustrating instances and investigate opportunities to change the game.

VALUES AND POLITICS

When we talk about value-driven people in organizations, we mean people who feel firmly bound to certain standards in attitudes and behaviors such as loyalty, honesty, openness, respect, fairness, justice, integrity, coexistence, and many more. Overall, we refer to the set of values we expect from exemplary members of an enlightened modern society, as reflected in legislation, moral standards, and common discourse. Some of these values are imposed on individuals by force, for instance, laws or social pressure through a social group or family, et cetera. Some are strongly internalized and form meaningful constituent elements of the identity of individuals.

Lawrence Kohlberg developed a theory of moral development in the 1950s that describes six stages, linked to three levels. His research suggests that only a small proportion of people will achieve level three of moral development—postconventional morality—that corresponds with the group of value-based people we refer to.

So what's wrong with being value-based in this way? In his book *The Fall of Public Man*, Richard Sennett describes a variety of psychological and sociological developments in people since the French Revolution that may help us to better understand the complex of problems around the issue at hand.

Before the French Revolution, in the *ancient regime*, the understanding of selfhood was fundamentally different from today. Much of an individual's identity derived from a person's public and private roles. Private roles were strictly limited to the closest family circle, allowing specific emotions, beliefs, behaviors, et cetera; they were also strictly separated from the public role. Public roles can be described by a common metaphor from the time, in which a person is seen as an actor playing a role on the stage called the world. We are equipped with a body, which we use as a puppet on this stage. Such a puppet must be dressed well in elegant costumes and must act in intelligent and brilliant ways, to earn the audience's admiration. Private roles were treated with the utmost discretion and were only visible to immediate family. At the time, it was fully acceptable to live two lives, a public life and a private life; these corresponded with divergent sets of values and behaviors, and neither society nor individuals bothered with discrepancies.

In that context, *political* still had a positive connotation. It captured all the possible skills, moves, and tactics that would help one to succeed in a challenge or competition in the public arena. Some ways and things were considered inappropriate, but these judgments related to the act rather than the actor's personality.

In today's thinking, an individual's personality is the ultimate core of knowledge. And identity! People spend much of their lives trying to find out who they are and which beliefs, values, attitudes, et cetera constitute their true selves. This true self is regarded the ultimate source of explanation for and understanding of one's being and ultimately also for understanding and judging others. Individuals in search of their real selves can end up navel-gazing or in a life-long introspective attempt to discover themselves. The true self is considered the holy grail of awareness.

THE CURSE OF AUTHENTICITY

This may explain the popularity of *authenticity*, which ranks high concerning assessing people across a range of situations and functions. We asked recently a client what he considers most important in his organization's leaders. His answer: Authenticity. In this context, we consider authenticity to be a myth. The doctrine of authenticity claims that everything individuals express to the world (inner or outer) must correspond to the person's true self; he or she will lose credibility if this is not the case.

As mentioned earlier there were times in our societies when the private role and the public role existed independently from each other. The concept of authenticity demands though that all—private and/or public—expressions of an individual—must be in accordance with the true self. This places a huge burden on those who have internalized this concept and limits their capability to act successfully in a political context more or less to zero. The concept demands concordance of things that simply do not go together. As a result, we can observe endless attempts by individuals to shape an anthropomorphic artifact that meets the demands of authenticity by either adapting the imagination or presentation of the true self to one's expressions, or by adapting the expressions of oneself in the private or public domain to what we have disclosed of our true self.

Foucault would certainly have included authenticity in his list of *dispositifs de pouvoir*—things that establish a certain distribution of power by influencing the social formations through the effects of discourse, applied (social) technologies or ideologies, because the authenticity dogma leads people to very favorable behavior from the perspective of people interested in power.

First, it keeps people focused looking inwards in ineffective attempts to get answers about their struggles, instead of looking outwards and investigating social and economic conditions. Second, it removes from individuals opportunities to act successfully in the public domain. Anyone committed to authenticity will be easy prey for those committed only to achieving their goals. This then can be, or most likely is, often diagnosed as the *political culture*.

Returning to our initial question: In our experience, why have the *good* never succeeded? First, because defeat is already built into their minds; second, as a result, they have not acquired the strategic or tactical skills to win or dare not apply them.

We will now introduce some cases from the business world and share what some masters of political skills might have advised in those situations. But this knowledge will be of no help unless we first overcome the preventing factors inside us. Stay committed to your values, but accept that your political moves are means to achieve and protect these values to the benefit of the organization and the people in it and to your own benefit! Authenticity as such is of no value in the context of leadership or in organizations generally. It only makes the people bend and twist psychologically to create a oneness where there is a multifaceted reality underlying multiple orders.

We analyzed what is available on and from the masters of politics. This does not imply that they were all and always value-driven, like our target group *the good ones*. We focus on what can make value-driven professionals more successful. We choose four masters one should learn from. Three are well known as statesmen, although few readers are likely to have read anything about or by them. They are: Machiavelli and the lesser known Giuccardini, Fouché, and Talleyrand. In their time, all four were what we would describe today as political savvy politicians. We will now briefly introduce our four protagonists.

Niccolò Machiavelli (1469–1527) was an Italian diplomat, politician, and historian who lived during the Medici years—the Renaissance—in Florence. He is widely known for his work *The Prince* and Machiavellism, a negative term to describe certain political behaviors. Many if not most people who associate Machiavelli with negatives such as putting the ends before the means have not read him and can learn from him.

Francesco Giuccardini (1483–1540) was a contemporary, friend, and critic of Machiavelli and had a similar background and experience. Unfortunately, he is not nearly as well known. Several experts consider his contributions to be at least of the same level and importance as those of Machiavelli.

Joseph Fouché (1759–1820) was a French statesman during the French Revolution and the minister of police under Napoléon. Historians often describe him as a clever but self-centered politician who could serve as a blueprint for opportunistic and political behavior. We see him as a skilled role-model for successfully managing difficult situations in today's business world.

Charles-Maurice de Talleyrand-Périgord (1754–1838) was a married, French bishop, statesman, and diplomat during the French Revolution, the time of Napoleon, and the Bourbon restoration. Similar to Fouché, he is associated with adaptability, opportunism, and political behavior. In our view, there is much to learn from Talleyrand, particularly on how to use diplomatic skills to succeed in organizations.

We do not judge these four based on the categories of morals or values, as *good* or *evil*.

In our view, managers can learn from them how power really works, how to be free to make the right decision, the approach to take in political situations, so as to be more successful, to win, to solve problems and to also bring a value-driven approach to fluxion.

We have chosen four typical situations that often occur in large organizations anywhere in the business world, and suggest an approach that might have been taken by one of the above mentioned four people. We believe that this third way—not opting out, not playing the game—will help not only *the good ones*, to not only survive, but also to be sustainably and successfully protect core values at the same time.

EXAMPLE 1: A MATRIX ORGANIZATION

How do I manage a situation in a matrix organization in which Boss A and Boss B do not get on and are trying to get at each other through me?

The setting: Being responsible for the finance function in the Latin America organization of my company, a global manufacturer of car parts, I have two bosses: the president of the Latin America organization and the global head of the finance function. I am colocated with my line boss in Buenos Aires, while my functional boss operates from global headquarters, in the United States

My functional boss visits regularly, and I am supposed to attend all relevant functional meetings outside my location. My line boss pushes me to focus completely on the success of his region. He orders me to ignore input from the function. My functional boss has the larger business in mind. She constantly tells me that it is my job to control my line boss and to ensure that the functional strategy is followed.

Accepting my responsibility and the dynamics of the matrix, I have tried to balance all aspects. However, this is not really working, and I increasingly feel caught in the middle.

What would be my next step? I will most likely invest time and effort in mediating between the two, trying to help them find common ground. I will likely try to avoid being exposed to any such situations. I might even ask a mentor or friend how to deal with this situation, to get—although unlikely—more ideas on what to do.

This will not work. Why? Because this tries to address an emotional issue with a rational cure. They know what they are doing is wrong, but they expose you to this situation anyway, because they have both a reason to do so, and because they can.

What would *the four* do? They would try to find an approach at the same level—aligning with the more powerful and influential of the two bosses. This reduces exposure by at least 50%, and gives one the possibility to influence that person to do what you think is right. After moving to his or her camp, their inclination to support you will increase by quite a margin.

EXAMPLE 2: CAREER PROGRESS

How can I be successful in a culture that pretends to reward performance and results, but is actually highly political and promotes people more or less based on personal relationships?

The situation: I am a marketing manager for a large confections brand in Europe. I am based in a small town in Switzerland and regularly travel to my markets, meeting my counterparts there, and providing them with knowledge and advice on how to better drive the brand in their local markets. I am also supposed to ensure that the brand equity is protected as much as possible against too many local modifications. I want to move ahead in the organization, and my next logical step would be to move into a marketing director role in one of the countries or to take over a much bigger brand at regional headquarters. There are regular talent planning meetings where my name is mentioned, at least I hope it is.

Most people in this situation would try to focus on doing a good job, so as to make this speak for itself. They also will most likely try to influence their boss and the human resource (HR) representative, the perceived influencers, more or less directly and more or less cleverly. There is nothing wrong with that. However, everyone else seeking to move ahead will do the same.

What might be the political savvy do? They would try to have a competitive advantage. *The four* would probably suggest finding out who influences the decision-makers and to impress them individually with what's important to each of them. They might be impressed by other things than your business skills or performance. The influencers might not visibly be the influencers. For instance, a decision-maker's administrative assistant tends to be very influential. A decision-maker's social partners can be very influential. Identifying and influencing by impressing them can give one the edge. *The four* might suggest doing this in a way that appears random but is planned to ensure that there are multiple opportunities for you to be mentioned in a positive light. Few of us are immune to the *halo effect*. It might be a good idea to also get more such references close to a talent planning event.

EXAMPLE 3: DECISION-MAKING

How do I manage successfully in a culture where decisions do not get made, owing to games among decision-makers, and where this constantly creates issues for me?

The frame: I work as a project engineer in a plant in China. Here, the assembly of the company's key product, a module for smartphones, is done, together with the production of key plastic molding components. My job is to implement new manufacturing equipment, in collaboration with all internal stakeholders, up to debugging the machines. From then, my production colleagues take over. To achieve my goal in the current production improvement program, I have to align my colleagues from purchasing, production, logistics, and finance. For various reasons, including personalities as well as functional constraints, they are not prepared to take the necessary decisions. So far, I have been moderating and driving the situation. I also compensate for the lack of progress by working harder and covering elements of their responsibilities myself. However, I have come to the conclusion that, if this continues, I will not deliver on time.

What might the "normal" approach be? Most people would probably approach their boss and ask for support. But would he or she be able, or prepared, to help directly or indirectly? In this case, it seems that the culture is such that making decisions is a challenge, so this might not lead to a true and comprehensive solution or significant progress.

What would the political approach be? Allow the larger organization to see what the consequences would be if this continued? Let something go wrong, and do not catch the "falling ball"; let it happen in a controlled way?. Do not allow someone to be harmed or hurt or the business to be significantly damaged, because this would come back to you. Let the flow of smaller well-contained problems create ripples and the dynamic that will then allow you to convince the decision-makers that this should never occur again. This would give you the facts—the related costs—to push for decisions.

If the organization, and your boss, is still not prepared to move, go as high as is necessary in the organization to make your case. It might damage your relationship with your boss, but it will build a new one with a more influential player. Queen trumps Jack.

EXAMPLE 4: A DIFFICULT BOSS

How do I succeed working for an extremely difficult boss?

The situation: I work as an HR business partner for the vice president, heading sales for Africa and the Middle East of my financial services company. I recently took over the job. As always you listened and have learned to better understand the business needs. I have met my internal and external customers and believe I understand where I can make a difference and support the senior leadership. The management team ranges from highly engaged in HR topics, with some appreciating my support a lot, to very passive and indifferent.

My boss has clearly shown that he plans to spend no time with you or to help me drive the HR agenda. He has not said so, but has indicated that his job is to drive the business, and nothing else. I have successfully worked with some of my internal customers and had hoped that this would convince him, but this has not happened. I have come to the conclusion that I must do something else.

Most people would probably focus on those in the organization who want the support. Or would get advice from the functional boss or other senior managers. Unless these managers are politically savvy, this will not help at all. Since the organization allows this boss to get away with such behavior, others' appetites to tackle the issue might be limited. It also bears the risk that the senior managers would talk among themselves, which might worsen your situation. It will become clear that you are in a victim role.

What would *the four* have done? They would probably suggest a different approach: Have a discussion with this boss along the following lines: Tell him that you do not want to continue as things are. Offer that in your functional role, you know that are a nuisance to him. Suggest that he should tell you what really motivates him in life; based on this, do only what supports this exact goal. If you learn that his sole motivation is his career, offer to would work only on HR topics that make him look good. If it is to bridge the year until retirement without too much trouble, offer to work around this, to allow this to happen. Thus, you will still be able to drive certain points on your agenda—perhaps not all, but more than before. You would also be demonstrating to him, and to others, that you are savvy, which should increase your influence. You would be winning the battle, and then the war.

These are four examples. We trust that they illustrate that different approaches can give difficult situations a completely different dynamic, often because they are different and unexpected. Taking such avenues would make us more tactical if not strategic and more successful without compromising on our values and intentions.

SOME NUGGETS FROM *THE FOUR*

To cover other potential situations, we have extracted some nuggets from *the four*.

Values and Skills

- You can be compassionate, loyal, humane, and honest, as long as you are mentally prepared to change as soon as your interests are threatened. You must understand that you cannot always behave in ways that would make people think you are good, because to stay in power, you are obliged to sometimes act against your values.

- A leader does not have to possess all virtuous qualities, but it is imperative that one seems to possess them. If you had them all, you might even put yourself at risk.

- Being silent makes you sympathetic. Being hard-working makes you admirable. Being invisible protects you against envy.

- A sensible leader cannot and must not keep their word if by doing so he puts themselves at risk and if the reasons that made them give their word are no longer valid.

- Never align with someone or something. Do not go with the idea; go with the times. Be with the winner, never the loser. Determine and declare yourself only when you know the winner. Then use the power and energy for your own endeavors.

- Deception is very useful, while frankness tends to benefit others rather than yourself. Since deception is not pleasant, use it only in very rare and important matters. Thus, you will have a reputation of being open and genuine and you will enjoy popularity that this brings. In these important matters, you will reap even greater advantage from deception, because your reputation for not being a deceiver will make your words easy to believe.

- You cannot always follow an absolute and fixed rule of conduct. Often it is unwise to be open. The only thing that makes others confide in you is their assumption that you confide in them.

- The highest art among all political skills is to let go at the right time. Do not fight lost causes.

Leadership

- Use force if necessary. Force is badly used when you are not drastic enough at the beginning but grow increasingly cruel later on rather than easing off. A leader who takes the first approach can improve their position; with the second approach, one has no such chance. Get cruelty over with as quickly as possible. When you have stopped using violence, you can win people with generosity.

- When you have to be aggressive to pursue your aim, do it in a way that the people executing it are seen as cruel, rather than you, so that you are not hated.

- To be successful, a leader must occasionally be very generous. That is enough. Hope is stronger than fear. They are more excited and pleased by the sight of one man well rewarded than they are frightened by seeing many men treated poorly.

- One thing to admire in successful leaders is how they involve people: They often ask questions without a concrete necessity. How could we approach this challenge? How would we do that? How would we go after this? A leader listens to people's ideas, expresses his own, and explains so much that this mental preparation helps to prepare everyone for the real-life situations that are then mastered.

- People will decide for themselves whether they love or fear a ruler, or not, while the ruler decides whether people will fear them. A sensible leader will base their power on what they control. But a ruler must take care that people do not hate them.

- If you do good things, you normally benefit only a few people at the cost of others. Then you will be vulnerable to the first bad news, and the first real danger will topple you. It is much safer to be feared than to be loved. People never forget fear of punishment.

- The only way to guard against flattery is to have people understand that you do not mind them telling the truth. But when everyone can tell the truth, you lose respect. A sensible ruler must find a middle way, choosing intelligent people for ministers and giving only them the right to tell the truth and only about the issues he or she asks about. However, a ruler should ask their ministers about everything, listen to their opinions, and make up their mind on their own, following their own criteria.

- There is one infallible way of checking a minister's credentials: when you see the minister thinking more for themselves than for you, when their actions are designed to enhance their own interests, they will never make a good minister.

Dealing With Challenges, Difficulties, and Difficult Bosses

- Moods will swing. It is easy to convince people of something, but hard to keep them convinced. So, when they stop believing in you, you must be in a position to force them to believe.
- Avoid open battle if possible, wait for others to make mistakes. Always spare enemies who can be useful to you.
- Be bold, never slow or hesitant in making decisions. Never give others time to think and position themselves. Be quicker than others.
- Waste no time with revolutions that do not remove the causes of your complaints but that simply change the face of those in charge.
- Nothing in life is more desirable or more glorious than to see your enemy prostrate on the ground and at your mercy. And the glory is doubled if you use it well, that is, by showing mercy and being content to have won.
- If you live under a tyrant, it is better to be his friend only to a certain extent, rather than be completely intimate with them. In this way, if you are a respected citizen, you will sometimes profit from their power even more than those closer to them. And if they should fall, you might still save yourself.

Influencing Others and Negotiations

- People generally judge more by appearances than first-hand experience, because everyone gets to see you, but few people deal with you directly. Those few do not have the courage to stand up to a majority opinion. People look at end results. So, if a leader does what it takes to win, they will always be considered honorable and will be praised. The crowd is won by appearances and final results.

- One of the greatest pieces of good fortune someone can have is the opportunity to make something they have done in their own interest appear to have been done for the common good.

- If you wish to communicate an important message with impact and to convince others, have the message conveyed by other people rather than delivering it yourself. People will listen more if they hear a message coming from more parties and others rather than from you.

- Always deny what you do not want to be known, and always affirm what you wish to be believed, because although there be much evidence, even conclusive evidence, to the contrary, a fervent affirmation or denial will often create at least some doubt in the mind of your listener.

- If you want to disguise or conceal an intention, always take pains to show you have its opposite in mind, using the stronger and most convincing reasons you can find. If people think you are reasonable, they will easily believe that your decisions will follow the dictates of reason.

- One way to make a supporter out of someone who would otherwise be hostile to a plan of yours is to make them think of it and to make them think they were its author or director. Light-hearted people are generally won over by this device, because it flatters their vanity, which is more important to them than real gains.

- Use rivalry among others to push them and at the same time control them. If you are not strong enough to quickly push for your will in larger groups of equals, destroy the unanimity and divide the group into camps. In this way, you can influence them better and can sometimes support this camp, and sometimes that one, depending on your goals.

- Avoid the marks of power and vanity. Being aware of power is sufficient. Work behind the scenes where you can influence and steer things. In this way, you will not be controlled and cannot be hated. One of the most powerful preventive measures against conspiracies is simply not being hated by a majority of people.

- It is a mistake to think that the victory of a cause depends upon its justice; we see the opposite every day. Not rightness, but prudent strength and good fortune bring victory. Having a just cause may be useful indirectly, but it is wrong to believe it can be of direct use. In short: Permitted is what is useful. The end justifies the means.

- This leaves us with the final question: How do we make this work in our everyday life?

Our recommendation is to try to find people who master such situations. There are always one or two in our direct environment. Observe them, or even ask them if they would mentor you. If you have the opportunity, get a coach: If you discuss a development goal with them, they can help you to get there. Find people outside of work that you can discuss difficult situations with without compromising confidentiality.

Read Machiavelli and Giuccardini! Read about Fouché and Talleyrand! Overcome the authenticity dogma inside of you! Forget about your true self and others' true selves.

Make yourself more successful. Bring your values to fruition and move beyond authenticity. If you do not do it for yourself, do it for the sake of your organization's culture.

CHAPTER 15

CONCLUSION

Emerging Lessons From Advanced Leadership Insights

Wolfgang Amann and Katja Kruckeberg

We have come to the end of our learning journey. We have presented you with a collection of emerging ideas that we deem to be of high importance for you as a current or future leader. We started off with insights for individuals who aspire to lead themselves to the pinnacle of success. We have looked at core questions for self-development, the role of persona & charisma for leaders, aspects to learn from neuroscience and the importance of mindfulness. In the next part of the book (Part I), we critically reviewed recipes for leading others to ultimate success. We revisited high-performance teams, state-of-the-art insights on negotiation and how to survive busy days and crises with the help of reflective leadership. We critically reviewed blue ocean leadership in the question why psychometric tools are still useful today.

Part III of the book zoomed in on navigating entire organizations through complexity. Our toolkit also included insights on stakeholder management and effective stakeholder dialogue. We proceeded with insights and suggestions for women in leadership by reviewing aspirations, obstacles as well as opportunities. We continued by encouraging

Advanced Leadership Insights: How to Lead People and Organizations to Ultimate Success
pp. 179–181

more transformational leadership and thinking big. While nowadays innovations can come from all corners from within organizations, leaders ought to do their part. We thus explored radical innovation and visionary leadership. Once such ideas and future success recipes have been developed, they need to be implemented. This book adds key thoughts on leaders as change-masters. Finally, in the last chapter of the book, we look at how to navigate the tricky waters of political games in companies, and prevent them from overwhelming the workload.

These chapters form the foundation of our "buffet of ideas" on advanced leadership insights. Throughout the book from the very beginning we emphasize that leaders are learners; and Ethos, pathos and logos continue to matter. How we design and implement solutions effectively strongly depends on however on a leader's ability to adapt to changing times (even driving change), shape ambiguous situations and doing so with the right goal in mind. No leader should be appointed without thorough ethical training. As we have outlined in this book, it is outdated to view staff members in a mere functionalist manner. Their well-being is an end in itself in a modern and humanistic understanding of what a company should achieve. Leadership is the means toward this end, and this does not equate ignoring economic realities.

Speaking of responsibilities of organizations and companies, we also want to take a clear stance on who should drive a leader's development. Organizations could conveniently defend that if a leader wants to be promoted, then s/he should bring along the necessary qualities—the business acumen, the leadership effectiveness, and the strong ethical and humanistic values. Individuals might well argue that expensive trainings are to be taken over by their employers so that they can focus on execution. In our worldview, this is a joint responsibility. Whatever gap an organization leaves should be filled by the individual and vice versa. There should not be any excuse for insufficient skills or training and development opportunities. The individual leader must therefore manage their organizations as much as organizations have to ensure that leaders have been soundly prepared and ready to lead. This book renders sensitive to key areas where a modern-day leader must have honed skills beyond self-awareness.

In this book, we also took a stance toward what leadership actually is. Some of our colleagues have published studies where 1,000, 3,000, or even up to 30,000 more or less different approaches to leadership have been addressed. Leaders are learners, while the very topic of learning is contingent upon each individual and the unique aspects of each situation. Despite claims to the contrary, working with psychometric tools and tests are not outdated in leadership development. They can not only boost self-awareness, but also open avenues for fundamental change.

Throughout this book we also emphasize that while each stage and transition for a leader requires them to adopt new skills and knowledge, it is also crucial to identify and consciously "unlearn" some of the success recipes that got them there—because successful learning is inevitably linked to unlearning. A personal performer, a line manager, a manager of managers, a manager of the function, a business (unit) leader or corporate or conglomerate leader will be challenged in a myriad of ways. This turns the speed of learning and overall readiness to embrace learning into key success criteria for ultimate success. Learning can emerge in various forms, including learning from failure. Individuals, teams and organizations should not be discouraged and demotivated from the inevitably recurring disappointments. They should be perceived as learning experiences to better create value for the well-being of stakeholders. We thus agree with Kegan and Laskow Lahey (2009) the too many leaders suffer from immunity to change and that a final test of greatness of leader can be found in the very way leaders evolve their mental complexity over time. Only then can we expect them to adequately cope with their organizations' internal and external complexity. Leaders early in their professional lives start with a very socialized mind. In order to be a good team player, they line themselves and follow the established, dominant logic of what great leadership, management and organizational development actually is. However, they free themselves self-authoring and rewiring the brains when they establish their own compress and agenda, when they drive their own learning. The ideal leader does not stop there. S/he ends up with a self-transforming mind that is characterized by eagerness to learn and evolve, readiness to accept ambiguities, empathy to see different stakeholder views and integrate different logics. After having learned how to lead, leaders learn how to learn best. You as the reader have taken a crucial first step. You have been exposed to reflection opportunities and hopefully several new ideas. You were invited throughout the chapters to practice in presented exercises and we encourage you to take one or two key thoughts from this book and experiment actively within your teams and organizations. We wish you good luck for your future leadership development journey!

REFERENCE

Kegan, R., & Laskow Lahey, L. (2009). *Immunity to change: How to overcome it and unlock potential in yourself and your organization.* Boston, MA: Harvard Business School Press.

ABOUT THE CONTRIBUTORS

ABOUT THE EDITORS

Wolfgang Amann is an award-winning professor of leadership and strategy, as well as the academic director of the custom, open, and degree programs at the Middle Eastern campus of HEC Paris in Qatar. Besides his doctorate in international strategic management from the University of St. Gallen, Prof. Dr. Amann has also graduated from all major faculty development programs worldwide, such as Harvard University's MLE, IMD's ITP, IESE, IFP, and EFMD International Deans Program. Wolfgang has published 30 books for executives and has compiled more than 100 case studies for his executive education seminars. He previously consulted for and trained executives, for instance, at China Development Bank, Daimler, Deutsche Bahn, Deutsche Telekom, Dixon/DSG, Dupont, the European Venture Capital and Private Equity Association, Evonik, Ford, Generali, Hilti, the UN, IBM, IFC/ Worldbank, Ikea, Marsoft, Mitsubishi, Office Depot, Tetra Pak, UNICEF, and W. L. Gore. Wolfgang has also been a guest professor at Hosei University (Tokyo), Tsinghua (Beijing), CEIBS (Shanghai), the Indian Institute of Management (Bangalore), ISP (St. Petersburg), Corvinus University (Hungary), Mzumbe University (Tanzania), Warwick Business School, Henley Business School (UK), and Wharton (U.S.). He has received numerous pan-European teaching awards and best lecturer recognitions. He repeatedly was honored with the Socially Responsible Faculty of the Year Award. During his academic direction of programs, HEC Paris in Qatar won the Enterprise Agility Award as well as the Entrepreneur of the Year 2015 Award, and the Educational Institute of the Year Award 2016 by Entrepreneurs Magazine.

Katja Kruckeberg is an international leadership consultant, facilitator, and keynote speaker who works with senior management on the human side of organizational change and strategy execution, across sectors. Dr. Kruckeberg (MBA, U.S.) has designed and delivered leadership development programs for top companies across the world, working with senior and middle managers from diverse cultural and industrial backgrounds for more then a decade. As a coach, she specializes in strength-based leadership development of organizations as well as high-performing teams and individuals. She has consulted for and trained executives, including at ABN AMRO, AcelorMittal, Alfa Laval, Airbus Group, Barilla, Canon Europe, Daimler, Commercial Bank of Qatar, Deutsche Bank, Deka Bank, Fujitsu, Generali Investment, Hypovereinsbank, Merck, Nokia, Nestle, Pirelli, Siemens, Shell, and Thyssenkrupp. As a leadership and personal development expert, she works with managers in both academic and corporate programs. Her many years of experience in management education include activities with other leading companies such as Frankfurt Business School (Germany), Duke C.E. (U.S.), IMD (Switzerland), St. Gallen Business School (Switzerland), HEC Paris (Qatar), Kinetic (Switzerland), and Kornferry International. For further information (in English and German), visit www.kruckeberg.de.

ABOUT THE AUTHORS

Maria Cristina Bombelli founded Wise Growth, a consultancy that specializes in diversity programs (www.wise-growth.it). After completing a degree in philosophy, she worked in a human resource department, focusing on training. A visiting scholar at the University of La Verne (CA) in 2004, Cristina was with the faculty at Bocconi School of Management for 22 years. In 2000, she founded Laboratorio Armonia, a companies network that researched diversity management. Cristina also was on the faculty of Bicocca University for 5 years. She has written several articles and books; these include *Women's Careers: The Long Road: All You Need to Know to Succeed* (2007), *Alice in Business Land: On Becoming a Woman Leader* (2009), *From Diversity to Plurality: A New Perspective on Organizational Inclusion* (2014), and *A Manager in the Middle Kingdom* (2015).

Tamara Carleton (PhD) is a global leader in helping organizations to create vision-led, radical innovations. She is the chief executive officer and founder of Innovation Leadership Board LLC and coauthor of *Playbook* *for Strategic Foresight & Innovation*, a hands-on guide used by hundreds of the world's most innovative companies to make their teams more successful. She also works closely with the Stanford Foresight research program at Stanford University in Silicon Valley. Dr. Carleton has served as a fellow with the U.S. Chamber of Commerce Foundation, the Foundation for Enterprise Development, and the Bay Area Science and Innovation Consortium. She was part of the Emerging Solutions practice at Deloitte Consulting LLP. She holds a doctorate in mechanical engineering from Stanford University and an MSc from Syracuse University. She is often invited to discuss her work in the United States and elsewhere. One can follow her on Twitter at @carleton.

William Cockayne (PhD) has led teams in incubation, research, product development, manufacturing, and shipping for more than 20 successful products at companies that include Eastman Kodak, DaimlerBenz, and Apple Computer. As an entrepreneur, Dr. Cockayne has created a number of pioneering products, including Lead|X (learning), the award-winning Travel by Handstand, Nota (education), and Change Research (analytics). As the cofounder and chief technical officer of Scout Electromedia, he has become famous. At Stanford University, he launched the ME410 course series Foresight & Technological Innovation, and works with companies around the world to convert visionary ideas into successful businesses. He holds a doctorate in mechanical engineering and an MSc in computer science, and is the inventor of multiple patents. He has authored numerous publications, including *Mobile Agents, free to download Playbook for Strategic Foresight and Innovation*, and the forthcoming *Playbook for Visionaries*.

Naysan Firoozmand, BSc (Hons) MSc C.Psychol AFBPsS, is managing director for Scandinavia and Netherlands at Ashridge Executive Education and Hult International Business School. He has extensive experience within both the private and public sectors and works with clients at organizational, team and individual levels to improve business performance through behavioral change. His areas of expertise include the design and delivery of leadership and personal development, cultural change, talent development, team building, and executive coaching. Naysan leads and manages project teams across the globe with a broad range of international clients. Before joining Ashridge Naysan was managing consultant for a European-based consultancy and client director for a Scandinavian leadership development firm. Naysan graduated with an MSc in occupational psychology and become a chartered psychologist in 2005. He is an associate Fellow of the British Psychological Society, a member of the Division of Occupational Psychology and a principle member of the Association for Business Psychology.

Marios Katsioloudes holds a PhD in management from the Wharton School, University of Pennsylvania, in strategy and international Business. He is currently a professor of management at Qatar University, where he teaches strategic management, international business, and entrepreneurship courses at the undergraduate and MBA levels. Throughout his 30-year career, Prof. Katsioloudes has worked for the Cyprus Development Bank and the World Bank. He has provided consulting services to small and medium-sized enterprises in Cyprus, the United States, Libya, Greece, the UAE, Saudi Arabia, and elsewhere. His research focuses on the strategic planning process in the for-profit and nonprofit sectors, entrepreneurship, and the management of change and innovation. He has (co)authored six books and has published more than 34 articles and 72 conference proceedings on strategic management, international business, and small business management/entrepreneurship. He is working on the second edition of his strategic management book, due for publication in 2016 by Routledge. He has also served as a member/chair of review panels for business programs in Bahrain, Oman, and Saudi Arabia.

Vicky Katsioloudes (PhD) is a human resource development professional with extensive experience in training and development in diverse cultural settings, including Cyprus, Greece, the United Kingdom, and the United States. She holds a PhD in human resource leadership development from Louisiana State University and an MSc in social and organizational psychology from the London School of Economics and Political Science. Vicky has taught undergraduate and graduate courses in leadership development, and her research interests include training transfer and leadership development. She is actively involved in the Academy of Human Resource Development and the Academy of Management as a presenter and reviewer.

Ragna Kirberg specializes in reflective leadership and communication. She serves as director of reflective leadership at Henley Business School and designs, directs, tutors, and coaches on leadership development programs for business transformation for leading organizations. She is also an executive coach. Her key driver is for individuals to become aware of and realize their potential. In her view, sustainable organizations empower their leaders to use the full potential of thinking and feeling. Ragna has worked with systemic and holistic approaches for many years; she combines this with more than 15 years of experience as an analyst and in leading investor relations positions, mostly with Allianz AG. During this time, she has won several awards. Ragna graduated from the University of St. Gallen (Switzerland), and was raised in Singapore and Bavaria.

Konstantin Korotov joined the European School of Management and Technology (ESMT) in August 2005 and received tenure in 2011. He is the director of the ESMT Center for Leadership Development Research (CLDR), which he cofounded with Prof. Manfred Kets de Vries. Prof. Dr. Korotov has authored, coauthored, and coedited six books and multiple academic and practitioner articles. He has won multiple awards for his case studies, articles, and teaching excellence. He is the program director for the ESMT executive programs Leading People and Teams and Leading with Psychological Intelligence. He teaches organizational behavior in the ESMT EMBA program and oversees ESMT EMBA students' Individual Leadership Development Itinerary. Konstantin's executive education portfolio includes programs for among others Siemens, Bosch, Daimler, ThyssenKrupp, Deutsche Telekom, E.On, RWE, EY, Axel Springer, KPMG, McDonald's, BAT, European Central Bank, Lufthansa, Symrise, Hereaus, Rosatom, Severstal, and Pernod-Ricard. He has also held the positions of director of professional development for Ernst & Young (CIS), consultant for the Center for Business Skills Development, and researcher at New York University.

Bernhard Küppers, based in Heidelberg, Germany, is a business angel, executive consultant, a member of supervisory boards, and a lecturer. In his long career as an executive board member, he was in charge of innovation and business development in a rapidly changing environment. He is the author of the book *Im Mittelpunkt steht der Mitarbeiter* (Haufe-Verlag) and the founder of ped-world. Bernhard also supports the Gründerinstitut of the SRH Hochschule Heidelberg and the European Foundation for Management Development (Brussels) as a peer reviewer for EQUIS and EPAS accreditation.

Ruth Ann Lake is a consultant and leadership development facilitator. She is American by birth, Italian through nationalization, and holds Lebanese nationality through family. After living and working for 3.5 years in Latin America, she pursued graduate work in Washington, DC, where she worked with in training programs sponsored by large multinational public sector organizations such as the OAS, IMF, World Bank, IDB, and others. She then moved to Italy where she worked for two major consultancies, leading various training and consultancy interventions, until she established her own company. Her topics of expertise include leadership and team-building, change management, cross-cultural management, and women in leadership. She is currently based in Nice, France and works internationally in English, Italian, Spanish, and French. She has published three books, on effective presentations, intercultural negotiations, and relational leadership. For further information (in English, Italian, French, and Spanish), visit www.ruthannlake.com.

Andreas Larsson is an associate professor and innovation leader at Blekinge Institute of Technology, and innovation practice advisor and case manager at MSF Sweden Innovation Unit (Médecins Sans Frontières/ Läkare Utan Gränser). He has worked with global product development and innovation for the past 15 years with companies such as Airbus, Rolls-Royce, GKN Aerospace, Volvo Cars, Sandvik Coromant, Getinge Infection Control, and BillerudKorsnäs. He is a former associate professor and subject head of innovation engineering at the Department of Design Sciences at Lund University (Sweden). Andreas holds a PhD in computer aided design at Luleå University of Technology (2005) and was a postdoctorate scholar at Stanford University's Center for Design Research (2008).

Tobias Mahr is an accomplished HR leader with a track record of extensive international experience as a strategic change consultant, translating business problems into HR solutions. He has more than 25 years of mainly international experience in consulting and the corporate world across Europe, the United States, and emerging markets. As a senior HR business partner with Gillette and Procter & Gamble, he gained experience in country, regional, and global roles. Tobias is an expert in strategy implementation, organizational transformation, talent and leadership development, and marketing and acquisition. His last assignment before joining Kinetic Consulting was in a senior European HR role with people responsibilities for about 14,000 employees in a global logistics company. Tobias lives in Berlin. His interests include wine, classical music, and history.

Felix Müller crosses boundaries between academia and practice to support people in leading the lives they want to live. He is the head of reflective leadership and management at Henley Business School Germany (Munich) and has more than 20 years of experience in senior leadership and management positions in international businesses such as PwC. Felix designs, directs, tutors, and coaches on leadership development programs for business transformation for leading organizations and is an executive coach. He holds a business degree from the University of St. Gallen (Switzerland) and an MBA from the Fuqua School of Business at Duke University, and is a candidate in the MSc in coaching and behavioral change at Henley Business School (UK). Felix's primary research interest is accessing the full potential inherent in every person, to lead a fulfilling life by aligning the head, heart, and gut. His research – at the intersection of psychology, sociology, and neurosciences—shows that reflection by thinking and feeling is a key factor for thriving in the increasingly challenging environment by doing what one really wants to do.

Matthew Mulford is an affiliate professor at HEC-Paris, a senior research Fellow at the London School of Economics, and a visiting faculty member at the European School of Management and Technology in Berlin. Dr. Mulford was a founding dean of the TRIUM Global Executive MBA program. TRIUM is a joint EMBA offered by New York University's Stern Business School, HEC School of Management in Paris, and the London School of Economics. The degree was ranked as one of the top five in the world by *Financial Times* in each of the years of his deanship. Prior to his deanship, Matthew was a senior lecturer in quantitative methods and negotiation analysis at the London School of Economics. His research interests include the psychology of judgment and decision-making, negotiation analysis, experimental game theory, and experimental research design. Dr. Mulford has designed, directed and/or taught executive training courses in more than 20 countries for a variety of clients.

Jim Shipley is originally from the United States, where he completed his master's in neuroscience. After a successful 20-year international career in leadership development, he returned to neuroscience and realized that insights about the human brain offer invaluable lessons about leadership. He has designed a 2.5-day program for senior leaders at ArcelorMittal using neuroscience insights as the framework for an intimate dialogue on leadership. Jim has been a member of GE's Global Leadership faculty since 2003, where he has received the Outstanding Faculty Award. He has also been invited to give keynote lectures on neuroscience and leadership. He is a member of the Neuroleadership Institute and lives in The Netherlands.

Bertolt Stein is recognized as a top-level executive coach and lead facilitator as well as an expert in organizational development, change management, and intercultural management. Dr. Stein has more than 20 years of experience in consulting across all industries, regions, and cultures, which makes him a very experienced global player. His main focus has been supporting leading international organizations, often over many years; these include Alcatel-Lucent, Johnson & Johnson, and Gillette (P&G). Although there are few areas he has not covered in his career, he has particular expertise in and a passion for leadership development, organizational/culture change, and executive coaching. Bertolt lives near Berlin. His interests include horse-riding, archery, and fly-fishing.